YORK NOTES

THE KITE RUNNER

KHALED HOSSEINI

NOTES BY CALUM KERR

 Longman

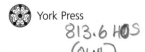 York Press

813.6 HOS
(OWL)

The right of Calum Kerr to be identified as Author of this Work has been asserted by him in accordance with the Copyright, Designs and Patents Act 1988

YORK PRESS
322 Old Brompton Road, London SW5 9JH

PEARSON EDUCATION LIMITED
Edinburgh Gate, Harlow,
Essex CM20 2JE, United Kingdom
Associated companies, branches and representatives throughout the world

First published 2009
Fourth impression 2010

ISBN 978–1–4082–1729–0

Phototypeset by Pantek Arts Ltd, Maidstone, Kent
Printed in China

CONTENTS

PART ONE

INTRODUCTION

STUDYING NOVELS

Reading novels and exploring them critically can be approached in a number of ways, but when reading the text for the first time it is a good idea to consider some, or all, of the following:

- **Format and style**: how do novels differ from other genres? How are chapters or other divisions used to reveal information? Is there a **narrator**, and if so, how does he or she convey both his or her emotions and those of the characters?

- **The writer's perspective**: consider what the writer has to say, how he or she presents a particular view of people, the world, society, ideas, issues, etc. Are, or were, these views controversial?

- **Shape and structure**: explore how the **narrative** of the story develops – the moments of revelation and reflection, openings and endings, conflicts and resolutions. Is there one main plot or are there multiple plots and sub-plots?

- **Setting**: where and when is the novel set? How do the locations shape or reflect the lives and relationships of the characters? What does the setting add in terms of tone?

- **Choice of language**: does the writer choose to write formally or informally? Does he or she use different registers for characters and narrators, and employ language features such as **imagery** and **dialect**?

- **Links and connections**: what other texts does this novel remind you of? Can you see connections between its narrative, characters and ideas and those of other texts you have studied? Is the novel part of a tradition or literary movement?

- **Your perspective and that of others**: what are your feelings about the novel? Can you relate to the narrators, characters, themes and ideas? What do others say about it – for example, critics, or other writers?

These York Notes offer an introduction to *The Kite Runner* and cannot substitute for close reading of the text and the study of secondary sources.

 CHECK THE BOOK

The Modern Novel by Jesse Matz (Blackwell Publishing, 2004) is a useful introduction to contemporary fiction written in both the UK and the USA.

READING *THE KITE RUNNER*

CONTEXT

On 11 September 2001, terrorists hijacked American planes and flew them into the two towers of the World Trade Center in New York and the Pentagon in Washington. This led to the USA and its allies invading Afghanistan later in 2001 in an attempt to find those responsible.

 CHECK THE NET

The website of the BBC, at **www.bbc.co.uk**, has many useful articles discussing the history of Afghanistan and the recent events there following the terrorist attacks in the USA on 11 September 2001. Go to the website and type 'Afghanistan history' into the search engine.

The Kite Runner is, to some extent, an **historical novel** in that a large part of its action is set in the past. Over the last 300 years many historical novels have been published with a variety of settings, from the Stone Age to very recent times. These settings are used by some writers as simple backdrops to create a particular mood for their book. Other writers use historical events as a source of inspiration for their story. With *The Kite Runner*, Khaled Hosseini has used the story to reflect on the historical events that surround it, but also uses this history to highlight the protagonist's journey.

Although much of *The Kite Runner* is set in the recent past, covering the last thirty to forty years, it also refers to events dating back as far as the Third Anglo-Afghan war of 1919, and the assumption of the throne by Zahir Shah in 1933. More details of the complex history of Afghanistan in the twentieth and early twenty-first centuries can be found in **Background: Historical background**.

The Kite Runner can also be seen as a **contemporary novel**. Since the events of 11 September 2001, international attention has been focused on Afghanistan and its political situation. This novel gives an insight into the path that has led to Afghanistan's current position and attempts to explore some of the less-well-known aspects of the country's cultural life.

Although large sections of *The Kite Runner* are set in the USA, it is intimately tied up with the culture of Afghanistan and its ethnic and religious groups, both as these exist in Afghanistan itself, and also as they exist in the wider world where Afghan refugees have congregated together. The study of fiction regarding immigrant groups living in other countries is one aspect of **post-colonial** literary theory, which is covered in the **Critical perspectives: Critical approaches** section of these Notes.

The **narrator** of *The Kite Runner* is Amir, an Afghan citizen who, as a boy, escapes the fighting in Afghanistan to travel with his father to the USA. He has grown into an adult in America and tells his story from this point of view. However, his story tells of events in his life from his early childhood through to his present time. The character is an author and he tells us his story in an attempt to understand and reconcile the events in his life and the relationships with the people around him. As such, both the historical setting and the location of Afghanistan could be seen as simple 'window dressing' to a quite traditional story. However, both the time and place are crucial to forming both Amir himself, and also his relationships with the people around him. As such, the setting is inseparable from the story.

Amir is telling his story as a way of redeeming the mistakes he made as a child, and to rid himself of the guilt he has felt ever since. He can be seen as an **unreliable narrator** because his view is skewed or biased by his personal feelings about the events he is relating. The novel should therefore be read with this in mind and the reader should attempt to decipher the reality of events from Amir's sometimes partial telling of the story. The use of the unreliable narrator is common in **postmodernism**. This is a literary movement which is also covered in **Critical perspectives: Critical approaches**.

As well as being an engrossing tale of a man growing up in the turmoil of Afghanistan and, later, as an immigrant in the USA, *The Kite Runner* is at times a challenging and disturbing novel. The main event of the novel is a dark and upsetting one, and later sections of it contain graphic descriptions of the treatment of Afghani citizens by the Taliban. Racial discrimination against the Hazara people by the dominant Pashtuns is also a theme. However, Hosseini does not use these elements simply to shock or to entertain, they are crucial elements in the formation of the characters of Amir, his father, Baba, and his friend, Hassan, and in the journey which Amir takes across the course of the novel.

The Kite Runner has had a remarkable success for what, on the surface, seems to be quite a simple and straightforward story. However, the time at which it was written – in the immediate aftermath of the 11 September attacks – and the subsequent wars in Afghanistan and Iraq, have made it a novel which has caught the public imagination. It contains much information which was new to readers in the West and provides an alternative, and more personal,

> **CONTEXT**
>
> The literary movement known as post-colonialism has grown up largely following the dismantling of the British Empire and the withdrawal of other colonial governments from a wide variety of countries. Inhabitants of these countries have used their new independence either to write about the experience of being colonised, or to move to the former colonising country and write about the experience from a distance.

 CHECK THE BOOK

The character of Stevens the butler in Kazuo Ishiguro's novel *The Remains of the Day* (Faber & Faber, 1989) is a classic example of an unreliable narrator. In one scene we find out that Stevens is upset and crying only because of the comments of other characters (p. 105).

CONTEXT

A kite runner is someone who runs after the free-flying kites which are produced when the string is cut during a kite fight. The rescued kite is kept by the winner of the fight as their trophy. Kite fighting is a popular sport in a number of eastern countries.

perspective to that provided by politicians and news organisations. In addition, it is a novel which encourages further research into the historical events described within it as well as being an engrossing personal tale of family and friends. As such, it is a rich text which rewards repeated readings and provides many different interpretations.

PART TWO

THE TEXT

NOTE ON THE TEXT

The Kite Runner was first published in 2003 by Riverhead Books, a division of Penguin Books (USA). It has been published in the UK by Bloomsbury Press Plc, London, in hardback and paperback; and in 2007 in a special edition to tie in with the recent film version. The 2004 Bloomsbury edition of the paperback was used in the preparation of these Notes. Audio, illustrated and e-book versions are also available.

The Kite Runner has been translated into forty-two different languages including Farsi, Hebrew, Russian, Korean and Chinese. In 2006 it was awarded the Penguin/Orange Reading Group (UK) Book of the Year prize; it has spent more than two years on the *New York Times* Bestsellers list.

SYNOPSIS

The Kite Runner is divided into twenty-five chapters and covers nearly thirty years of time. It begins in December 2001 with the main character and **narrator**, Amir, remembering a phone call from the previous June. Amir is an Afghan emigrant who now lives in San Francisco. The phone call was from an old friend of his father, a man called Rahim Khan, who asked Amir to come to Pakistan to see him. This triggered memories of Amir's childhood and he now proceeds to relate the story of his life.

Amir and his father, Baba, live in a large house in a prosperous part of Kabul. They have two servants, Ali and his son, Hassan. Amir's mother is dead, having died giving birth to her son. Ali's wife is also absent, having run away just five days after Hassan's birth. Ali and Hassan are part of a minority ethnic group in Afghanistan, the Hazara, and are looked down on because of this. Baba and Amir belong to the Pashtun, the majority group.

CHECK THE NET

The author's own website, **www.khaled hosseini.com**, contains information about the successful publishing history of this novel.

CHECK THE FILM

A film of *The Kite Runner* was released in 2007. Although the opening is somewhat different to that of the novel, it is a remarkably faithful adaptation.

? QUESTION
In the opening section of the novel Amir and Hassan are portrayed more like brothers than friends. What is the significance in the novel of their varying relationship?

Amir and Hassan are constant childhood companions playing together and getting into trouble together. Whenever trouble arises, however, whether it is a scolding from Ali or being threatened by bullies, it is Hassan who always protects Amir rather than the other way around: on one occasion he threatens a bully called Assef with his slingshot.

Baba is a greatly respected member of Kabul society, partly for his talent for business, but largely for his charismatic personality. Amir, however, is something of a disappointment to him, lacking his self-confidence and love of sports. Amir's interests lie instead with the written word. He often reads stories to Hassan and, one day, makes up his own. Hassan likes it so much that Amir starts to write down his stories. His father is not impressed, but Amir gets encouragement from Rahim Khan.

The one thing which brings Amir and his father together is kite fighting. Amir is an accomplished kite fighter and Hassan is very talented at predicting where the defeated kites will land, making him the 'kite runner' of the novel's title. Each winter in Kabul there are kite-fighting tournaments and in 1975 it is being held in Amir's neighbourhood. Amir sees this as a good chance to impress his father. He wins the tournament and Hassan runs for the final defeated kite, but fails to return. When Amir goes in search of Hassan he finds him trapped in an alley by a group of bullies, one of whom is Assef, who proceeds to rape the young servant. Amir is too frightened to do anything to help and runs away.

CHECK THE BOOK
Another novel in which a key event in the **narrator's** childhood affects the rest of their life is *Great Expectations* by Charles Dickens (1860–1).

The event in the alley is never mentioned, but Amir's guilt leads to him shunning Hassan's friendship and finally to him framing Hassan for theft. As a result Ali and Hassan leave Baba's house, much to Baba's distress. Amir's guilt continues to affect him for the rest of his life.

The story moves to 1981 and Baba and Amir are forced to escape Hassan from an Afghanistan which has been invaded by the Russian army. They make their way to Pakistan and then on to the USA where they settle in Fremont, California. Once there Baba takes whatever jobs he can get while Amir goes to high school and then on to college to study creative writing. They spend their weekends buying items from garage and lawn sales and then selling them on from a stall in the Afghan section of the San Jose flea market, a place where Baba can mingle with his own people. It is at this market that Amir meets his future wife, Soraya.

Baba falls ill with what turns out to be lung cancer. Amir and Soraya marry swiftly and she helps Amir nurse his father during his final weeks. The young couple then move into their own house and try to start a family but find that they are infertile. At the same time Amir meets with success in his writing, securing a publishing deal for his first novel.

Then, in June 2001, Rahim Khan calls Amir. He informs Amir that he can finally make up for the events of the past, so Amir goes to Pakistan to see him. Rahim Khan has left Kabul to come to Pakistan because he is seriously ill and dying. He wants to see Amir one last time and to ask a favour of him, but first he relates the story of his life since they last saw each other.

Rahim Khan remained in Baba's house even during the Russian invasion and the subsequent rule of the Taliban. When he learned of Baba's death, a feeling of loneliness led to him seeking out Hassan. Rahim Khan found him and brought him and his wife back to Kabul to live with him. Shortly afterwards, Hassan's mother returned and lived with them for the four years until her death, becoming part of the family once again. Hassan's wife gave birth to a boy named Sohrab. When his illness struck, Rahim Khan determined to come to Pakistan for medical help. Shortly afterwards both Hassan and his wife were executed by the Taliban.

Rahim Khan does, however, have a letter for Amir from Hassan and a favour to ask of him. Sohrab has been placed in an orphanage in Kabul and Rahim Khan wants Amir to retrieve him and place him with a foster family in Peshawar. At first Amir refuses but then Rahim Khan reveals that Hassan was actually Baba's son, not Ali's, and therefore Hassan was Amir's half-brother. This makes Sohrab Amir's nephew.

Amir finally agrees, seeing a chance to lay his demons to rest, and travels in disguise back to Kabul. The country, and the city, have been devastated by nearly thirty years of war. Amir finds the orphanage but Sohrab has been sold to a high-ranking member of

CONTEXT

Kite flying was banned in Afghanistan by the Taliban, an extremist Islamic group who imposed their strict interpretations of Sharia Law on the country from around 1994 until removed from power by the Northern Alliance and NATO forces in late 2001. They were renowned for their violence, extreme punishments and poor treatment of women.

QUESTION
The whole of the story of Amir's return to Afghanistan examines the idea of 'unfinished business'. Amir is finally forced to grow up by dealing with the events of his childhood that he previously ran away from. In what way does Assef represent this idea?

the Taliban. The next day Amir finds the Taliban member stoning people to death during the half-time break at a football match. Amir arranges to meet the man, who does indeed have Sohrab, but who then reveals himself to be Assef, the bully who raped Hassan all those years ago.

Assef tells Amir that he can take Sohrab but he needs to fight for him. Amir agrees and suffers a terrible beating. He is saved, however, by Sohrab shooting Assef in the eye with his slingshot.

As Amir recovers in Peshawar, he discovers that there is no adoptive family for Sohrab and so he offers to take the boy back to the USA. However, when this proves problematic he admits that Sohrab might need to go back into an orphanage for a time. This so upsets Sohrab that he attempts suicide.

Amir does manage to take the boy back to the USA with him, but the trauma that Sohrab has suffered leaves him mute and unresponsive. He is finally brought out of himself at the end of the novel when he and Amir successfully engage in a bout of kite fighting in a Fremont park.

Detailed summaries

Chapter 1

- Amir, the Afghan narrator of the novel, now lives in San Francisco.
- Amir has received a phone call from his father's old friend, Rahim Khan, asking him to come to Pakistan.
- The phone call has reminded Amir of events from his past.

The Kite Runner opens with Amir, the **narrator** and main character of the novel, looking back six months to the summer of 2001 when he received an unexpected phone call from an old friend of his father. This phone call stirred a memory from twenty-six years earlier, in the year 1975, and made him recall an unspecified event which he watched in an alley. He took a walk in Golden Gate Park in San Francisco, where he now lives, and saw kites being flown. They reminded him of his boyhood friend Hassan, a kite runner with a cleft lip, and he remembers how the events of 1975 moulded him as a person.

COMMENTARY

This novel is mostly narrated by its central character, who we find out at the end of Chapter 2 is named Amir. This is a **first-person narrative** wherein we see only Amir's perspective of events rather than those of the other characters. This means that the events we are shown in the novel are all coloured by Amir's personal reactions and emotions rather than being from an objective viewpoint.

The short opening chapter acts as a double frame for the story to come. Although the story is being told in December 2001, we are immediately referred back, first to a phone call in the previous summer, and then to events that occurred in 1975. The rest of the story is therefore told as a series of extended **flashbacks**. The narrator is talking to us after the end of the story at a point where he already knows how it ends, and this fact colours the rest of the narrative. Such a technique allows the narrator to **foreshadow** events which have not yet occurred, building **dramatic tension**.

Four other characters are mentioned in this chapter – Rahim Khan, Hassan, Hassan's father, Ali, and Amir's father, Baba. The inclusion of these names in this short first chapter confers significance upon them so the reader knows that they are key characters in the narrative to come.

Kites are also mentioned in this chapter, immediately reinforcing the novel's title. The sighting of them in San Francisco is what links Amir back to his memories of Kabul; he then connects them by thinking of Hassan, whom he names 'the harelipped kite runner' (p. 1). This identifies Hassan as the kite runner of the title and lets the reader know that of the characters mentioned, Hassan will be the most significant for the progression of the story.

CONTEXT

The novel opens by **juxtaposing** Amir's memories of Afghanistan with his current life in the USA. This is reinforced by the iconic image of San Francisco's Golden Gate Bridge. The bridge was built between 1933 and 1937 and has since become an internationally recognised symbol for San Francisco, California and America as a whole.

 CHECK THE FILM

The technique of narrating a story through 'flashback' is very common in films. One of the earliest, and most famous, uses of this technique was in the 1941 Orson Welles film *Citizen Kane*, in which the film opens with Kane's death and the story of his life is told in a series of flashbacks.

The language that Amir uses when he recalls the past carries much emotion. He talks about 'burying' the past and how it 'claws its way out' (p. 1), invoking an **image** of something dead rising from its grave. He also recalls words from his phone call with Rahim Khan, '*There is a way to be good again*' (p. 2). The inclusion of this line suggests that the events of the past include something for which Amir needs to atone; in other words, the tale to come involves him; seeking redemption for earlier actions. We are not yet told what these actions might be, but the repeated mention of 'peeking into the alley' (p. 1) in Kabul in 1975, again acts to **foreshadow** events and informs the reader that this is a key incident in what unfolds.

Another language technique employed here is **pathetic fallacy** where the weather is used to reflect the character's feelings. In this case, the day in 1975 when his life changed is described by Amir as 'a frigid overcast day' (p. 1) reflecting the oppressive and chilling emotions he experienced then.

GLOSSARY

1 **frigid** cold, icy, also lacking in affection or warmth of feeling

1 **harelipped** a birth defect where the lip and/or the palate of the baby have not fused. This leads to a gap in the upper lip. The term harelipped is no longer used, with 'cleft lip' or 'cleft palate' being preferred

2 **Kabul** capital city of Afghanistan

CHAPTER 2

- Amir looks back and remembers how he and Hassan were childhood friends despite Hassan being the son of Amir's family's servant, Ali.

- We learn that Amir's mother died in childbirth.

- Amir recounts how Hassan's mother abandoned her family shortly after giving birth to him.

- We learn that the families of Amir and Hassan are from two different ethnic groups.

Amir describes how he and Hassan played together as children, annoying the neighbours and their dog, and how Ali, Hassan's father, would catch and reprimand them. He explains how in such situations Hassan would take the blame rather than pass it onto Amir.

Amir's house was built by his father, Baba, with Ali and Hassan living in a hut in the grounds. Hassan was born in that hut just one year after Amir's mother died giving birth to him. Hassan's mother, much younger than Ali, left her husband just five days after giving birth to Hassan. She had always had a reputation as a flirtatious and potentially unfaithful woman and Amir relates an occasion when Hassan was recognised by a soldier who claimed to have had sex with her. Ali suffered from polio, and Sanaubar was very beautiful, so the assumption was that it had been an arranged marriage because people could not understand how else he might have persuaded her to marry him. Ali was a Hazara, a lower caste, or class, in Afghanistan, and was often taunted in the streets because of this. Amir discovers in a history book that the Hazara, who are Shi'a Muslims, had long been persecuted by his own people, the Pashtuns, who are Sunni Muslims. When he shows the book to a teacher, the teacher dismisses this idea.

Finally, Amir tells of his kinship with Hassan, how they shared the same wet nurse, and how Amir's first word was 'Baba', while Hassan's was 'Amir'. He adds that the events of 1975 were founded in these first words.

COMMENTARY

Chapter 2 takes us back to events of Amir's childhood and immediately introduces us properly to the character of Hassan. Following the indication of his significance in Chapter 1, the way in which he is drawn in Chapter 2 shows us the importance of Hassan not just to the Amir of the past, but also to the man he has become.

Amir describes his old friend using poetic imagery – 'a face like a Chinese doll chiseled from hardwood ... eyes that looked, depending on the light, gold, green, even sapphire' (p. 3) – which reinforces the expression of the love that he still feels for Hassan. This use of lyrical language occurs throughout the novel, often

> **CONTEXT**
> Polio, officially Poliomyelitis, is an acute viral infectious disease. It affects the central nervous system and causes muscle weakness and paralysis. A vaccine for the virus was famously developed in 1952 by Jonas Salk, with another being produced shortly thereafter. This has led to a radical cut in the number of cases of polio worldwide. One of the countries where the infection is still active is Afghanistan.

> **CONTEXT**
> Amir refers to Hassan as having 'a face like a Chinese doll' (p. 3). This is Hosseini's way of referring to Hassan's different ethnicity. Being Hazara, Hassan would have had distinctive facial features, with a flatter nose and narrower eyes than the Pashtuns around him, similar to the Mongolians or the Chinese.

associated with significant characters such as Hassan, but also with key places such as the Kabul of Amir's childhood memories.

Amir relates the times when he and Hassan would get into trouble and how, when they were caught, Hassan would take the blame for their antics. This sets the mould for events to come, including Amir's later reaction to the crucial event in the alley. It shows how their relationship is based on Hassan's unquestioning loyalty to his friend, and Amir's somewhat more uncertain feelings about a friend who is also a servant. This is further reinforced when Amir reveals the boys' first words: Amir's was his father's name, and Hassan's was his friend's name.

This chapter also introduces us, for the first time, to Baba, Amir's father, who is a powerful man. Amir explains how he wished to spend time with his father, but that Baba would ask Amir to leave and 'read one of those books of yours' (p. 4). Just as Amir's descriptions of his experiences with Hassan set a pattern for the rest of their interactions, so his first descriptions of his father do the same thing. We are shown an early indication of Amir's quest for his father's approval, and the way in which Baba views Amir's intellectual abilities as being a sign of weakness.

We are also told in this chapter of the fate of Amir's and Hassan's mothers, Sofia and Sanaubar. The role of women in this novel is largely characterised by their absence, with the lack of mothers and wives making the relationships between Amir, Hassan, Baba and Ali all the stronger. The relevance of the descriptions of Hassan's mother's overt sexuality and her treatment of her husband are revisited later in the story.

Among the introduction of key characters and the description of childhood events in this chapter, we are given our first insight into the roles of ethnicity and history which play a large role in what unfolds in the novel. Ali and Hassan are part of the 'Hazara' ethnic group which is seen as being inferior to the 'Pashtun' group of which Amir and his family are a part. We are told about the teasing and taunting of the Hazaras which Amir has witnessed and the book in which he has found records of the persecution and oppression of the Hazara by the Pashtuns. The fact that Amir finds this information in a book which belonged to his mother, but that its contents are dismissed by his teacher, shows the difference between the way Amir is brought up

CONTEXT

Ali sings a song to Amir and Hassan about their kinship. It is a song about Ali, the Lion of God, who was a cousin of the prophet Muhammad, and the cause of the split between Sunni and Shi'a Muslims. The Sunni, the largest branch of Islam, are defined by their belief that any of the first four successors to Muhammad (Caliphs), and their descendants, could be seen as legitimate leaders of Islam. The Shi'a are the minority branch of Islam, who believe that only Ali, the fourth Caliph, and his descendants, are the real successors to Muhammad.

to view the Hazara and the way that most Afghanis view them. This is a theme which continues throughout the novel.

GLOSSARY

4	**Wazir Akbar Khan** wealthy suburb of Kabul, named after Mohammad Akbar Khan who led a revolt against the British occupation of Afghanistan in 1841
4	**Isfahan** a large city in Iran
5	**King Nadir Shah** king of Afghanistan from 1929 until his assassination in 1933
5	**loquat tree** an evergreen fruit tree; distant relative of the apple tree
6	**Herati rug** a rug from Herat, a city in western Afghanistan
6	*Allah-u-akbar* Arabic for 'God is great/the greatest'
6	**Mashad** a large city in Iran
6	**hemorrhaged** bled
6	**Istiqlal** Arabic for 'independence'
7	**elope** run away, usually to run away to marry in secret
7	**unscrupulous** lacking a sense of what is right
7	**congenital** a defect or illness present at birth due to inherited or environmental factors
7	**atrophied** wasted away from disease or lack of use
7	**bazaar** a Middle Eastern street market
7	*naan* an Indian flatbread
9	**garrulous** given to talking a lot
9	**Bamiyan** the largest town in Hazarajat in central Afghanistan, an important location for Buddhism

---

CHAPTER 3

- Amir remembers time spent with his father during his childhood, and how his father was disappointed with his lack of manly attributes.

- Amir's father, Baba, was seen as a great man by the people around him.

- Amir recalls becoming interested in reading and writing as a way to escape his father's lack of interest.

- Amir takes out his resentment and jealousy on Hassan.

 CHECK THE NET
Information about the Hazara people and their history can be found in the article 'Afghanistan's outsiders' on the National Geographic website. Go to **http://ngm. nationalgeographic. com** and search for 'Hazara'.

CONTEXT

Fights with bears and beasts are a common way of showing bravery (or cowardice) in literature. Baba compares well with Antigonus in Shakespeare's play, *The Winter's Tale*, who famously exits the stage 'pursued by a bear' (III.3.57), but in that case is killed by it.

Amir recounts the story of his father wrestling a black bear and how he has three large scars to prove it. Rahim Khan's nickname for Baba was 'Mr Hurricane'. These details show, according to Amir, how impressive a figure his father was. When Amir was five or six, his father decided to build an orphanage despite many people saying he did not have the skills. He succeeded and all the sceptics were impressed, and Amir was immensely proud. On the day before the orphanage opened Baba took Amir to Gargha Lake for a picnic lunch. Baba had wanted Hassan to come too, but Amir had lied and said Hassan was ill because one time, on a trip to the lake, his father had put his arm around Hassan and patted his head. On the day of the opening, Baba's hat was blown off during his speech and Amir was pleased to hold it so that people could see he was this great man's son.

The pattern of Baba doing things which people thought beyond him continued. People thought he couldn't run a business. In reply he became a rich merchant running a carpet-exporting business, two pharmacies and a restaurant. People thought he would not marry well. He married Amir's mother, Sofia Akrami, a beautiful, respected, intelligent woman descended from royalty, and also a teacher of literature.

QUESTION
Amir portrays himself as different from his father, more free-spirited and Western in his approach, but it is clear from discussions such as the one they have about alcohol and religion that Baba is more liberal than Amir sometimes admits. How does this affect your reaction to Amir as a character and a narrator?

Amir sees himself as the only thing his father could not mould to his desires. One night, in Baba's study, he told his father about the lesson he had learned in school that drinking alcohol was a terrible sin. Baba's response was to scorn the religious teachings that Amir was repeating and to teach Amir his own interpretation of scripture: 'there is only one sin, only one. And that is theft. Every other sin is a variation of theft' (p. 16). He explained this comment by the examples of murder being theft of a life and cheating being theft of fairness. Amir finally understood this and realised he stole the life of his mother by killing her during childbirth. He believes that his father hates him for this.

We learn that at school Amir became interested in poetry and escaped his father's lack of interest by reading his mother's books. His father tried to interest him in sports and traditional male activities. One year he took him to a Buzkashi tournament and they saw one of the *chapandaz* (a jockey) thrown from his horse and trampled to death. Amir's response was to cry all the way home. That evening he overheard his father talking with Rahim Khan. Baba commented that when Amir is bullied on the street he doesn't fight back. Instead, Hassan steps in and fights for him. On returning home Amir will then lie about how Hassan got his injuries. Baba's final comment was that he finds it hard to believe Amir is his own son. The next morning Amir snapped at Hassan in retaliation for the things he heard his father say about him.

COMMENTARY

Amir continues relating stories from his childhood with the tale that his father once wrestled a black bear. The nature of this story reinforces the **image** created in the previous chapter of Baba as a strong, powerful man. It also sets the theme for this chapter, which is the love and pride that Amir feels for his father, and also the awe which his reputation creates.

The story of Baba's building of an orphanage shows his father as a benefactor, a man of action and as being kind to children. However, the way Amir relates the story also highlights the poor relationship between him and his father and his jealousy at the way Baba interacted with Hassan. This passage is discussed in greater depth in **Extended commentary 1**. Amir continues by telling other stories of Baba's great stature, emphasising his ability to do those things of which other people considered him incapable. In this way, Amir paints his father as almost a mythological figure rather than a real man. His subsequent desire to live up to his father's wishes is therefore revealed as ultimately futile because his goal is a myth rather than a reality.

When Amir confronts his father about his drinking Baba, talking of the religious leaders, says 'God help us all if Afghanistan ever falls into their hands' (p. 15). This **foreshadows** the later rule of the Taliban in Afghanistan, and injects a note of warning and future tragedy, even at this early point in the story.

CHECK THE FILM

Omar Khayyám (p. 17) was a Persian mathematician, astronomer and poet who was born in the eleventh century. His collection of love poetry, the *Rubaiyat of Omar Khayyám*, composed entirely of quatrains (four-line stanzas), is also famous in the West for its beauty and simplicity, and is often compared to the works of Shakespeare for its influence on later writing.

CHECK THE BOOK

In his book *The Hero with a Thousand Faces* (1949), Joseph Campbell examines mythic structure for common elements. One which he identifies is the process of achieving 'atonement with the father'. Amir's need to do this is just one of the ways in which his journey matches Campbell's scheme.

The principle of *zakat* (p.14), a custom whereby Muslims are expected to give a specified percentage of their yearly income to charity is the method by which the poor receive welfare in Afghanistan.

Finally in this chapter, the story of going to the Buzkashi tournament emphasises the differences between Amir and his father and also between the boy his father wishes him to be and the boy he really is. Baba's statement that he cannot believe Amir is his son forms a foundation for the story of the relationship between the two, with Amir's story being one of striving to make his father proud of him. And, in the last small section of the chapter, we see for the first time how Amir's desire to please Baba manifests itself in cruelty to Hassan. Amir identifies this cruelty as evidence of the 'mean streak' (p. 20) Rahim Khan claimed he didn't possess.

CONTEXT

Buzkashi (p. 18) is a very popular sport in all of central Asia. The players spend many years learning to master the sport and the specially trained horses are traded for substantial amounts of money.

GLOSSARY

11	**Baluchistan** a region which covers parts of Pakistan, Afghanistan and Iran
12	**Ghargha Lake** a lake near Kabul
12	*kofta* spiced meatballs
12	**hippies** members of the counter-cultural movement of the late 1960s
14	**Farsi** a Persian language spoken in Iran, Afghanistan and Tajikistan
14	**mullah** a Muslim cleric
14	*hadj* an annual pilgrimage to Mecca, the holiest city in Islam
14	*namaz* the Islamic prayer which is performed five times a day
14	**Koran** the Islamic holy book
15	**Genghis Khan** feared founder and emperor of the Mongol Empire in the twelfth century
16	**Kunduz** a city in northern Afghanistan
17	**Khayyám, Hāfez, Rumi and Saadi** Persian poets
18	**aficionado** someone with a passion for and wide knowledge about an activity
18	**Henry Kissinger** Secretary of State in USA, 1973–7, under Richard Nixon's and Gerald Ford's administrations

CHAPTER 4

- We learn how Ali, Hassan's father, was an orphan raised by Baba's father.
- When they were growing up, Hassan acted as Amir's servant.
- Amir recalls writing his first story.

Amir's father was born in 1933 and, in the same year, Ali's parents were killed in an accident and Baba's father took the five-year-old boy in and gave him to the servants to bring up. Ali and Baba then grew up together, just as Amir and Hassan did years later. However, Amir comments that he never heard Baba refer to Ali as his friend, and realises that he never thought of Hassan as his friend either. The reason he sees for this is religion. Amir is a Pashtun – a Sunni Muslim – and Hassan a Hazara – a Shi'a Muslim.

Despite this division, Amir recalls that they spent a happy childhood together, playing, exploring and learning about the world. During the school year Amir would get up and Hassan would already be awake and have prepared Amir's breakfast. Hassan would make Amir's bed and prepare his clothes and pack his school bag for him while he ate. Amir would then go to school and Hassan would stay at home cleaning and cooking. After school they would climb a hill to an old cemetery where one day Amir carved their names on a pomegranate tree. They would sit there, under the tree, and Amir would read stories to his illiterate friend.

Amir would read simple stories that he felt his friend could understand and would tease him if he did not know a word. Their favourite story was 'Rostam and Sohrab' in which a great warrior mortally wounds his greatest enemy who turns out to be his long lost son. One day, as a trick, Amir invented his own story instead of reading the one in the book. He was surprised when Hassan applauded it as the best story he had heard in a long time. That night Amir wrote his first story in which a man murders his own wife in an effort to gain riches but discovers that riches cannot replace the happiness he has lost by killing her. He took the story to his father, but Baba did not offer to read it. Instead, Rahim Khan

CONTEXT
The year of 1933 is crucial as the year of Baba's birth, and the year that Zahir Shah started his forty-year peaceful reign of Afghanistan, but also as the year that Adolf Hitler was appointed Chancellor of Germany.

took it and read it. Rahim Khan gave him a very positive response and so Amir went downstairs, woke Hassan and read it to him. Hassan loved the story but identified a possible hole in the plot. Amir's response was one of anger and spite. Before he could voice these feelings, however, Amir tells us that at that moment, 'Afghanistan changed forever' (p. 30).

COMMENTARY

As Amir relates the story of how Ali came to be his father's servant he draws a comparison with his own relationship with Hassan. He also provides a way of explaining the difference between himself and his father, and Ali and Hassan, on the basis of their religion.

The films Amir and Hassan go to see at the cinema are mostly Westerns. This is our first mention of the West in the young Amir's story, and again connects us with the older Amir telling the story from his new home in the USA. The **motif** of the Western as a film genre is also relevant, with its clear delineation of good guys and bad guys and justice winning out. Actors like John Wayne can be seen as being similar to Baba in the way Amir looks up to both them and his father as larger-than-life figures.

In this same section we are given rich descriptions of Kabul which evoke the many smells, colours and noises of the city. These are important in providing a setting for the events of Amir's childhood but also provide a basis for comparison when we are presented with a much-changed Kabul later in the novel.

Amir's reading to Hassan seems a friendly and compassionate act, reminiscent of his mother being a teacher. However, Amir does not teach Hassan to read and therefore retains his power over the servant. He is then in a position to use this power against Hassan by teasing him and teaching him the wrong meanings to words.

The boys read in an old cemetery under a pomegranate tree. The disused cemetery represents both a place of death, but also, because it is disused, a place beyond both death and life. It is a refuge, a place where the real world cannot reach them. The pomegranate tree, bearing sweet fruits full of seeds, is **symbolic** of life and plenty, but also of the sweetness of the bond between the two boys who share the fruit before Amir reads to Hassan. The cemetery and the tree are symbols which return throughout the novel.

Stories themselves are a central motif in the novel. Most of the novel is a story being told to us by Amir, rather than an objective tale being told by a third-party **narrator**. Within that larger story we see Amir read stories to Hassan. At first he adds to and amends them, and finally he moves on to writes his own stories. This creates a bond between him and his dead mother, who was a teacher of literature. However, it also gives him the tools to express feelings which have no outlet. In the first story he writes he creates a scenario which is described by Rahim Khan as **ironic**, but also one which is sad and disturbing. This provides an outlet for his own feelings and a mirror by which we can examine them. In response to Amir's story, Hassan spots a plot hole, showing his ability to see things clearly as opposed to Amir's more muddied and emotional thinking. Amir's 'mean streak' once again appears as he asks himself, *'What does he know, that illiterate Hazara? He'll never be anything but a cook'* (p. 30).

CONTEXT

Mullah Nasruddin (p. 24) supposedly lived in Turkey in the thirteenth century. Stories of his actions have passed into folklore in a number of countries including Iran, Turkey, Uzbekistan and Afghanistan. He is known as a 'wise fool'.

 QUESTION
Examine Amir's first short story in the context of the whole of the novel. What does it reveal about his character?

GLOSSARY

21	**Zahir Shah**	the last king of Afghanistan, reigning 1933–73
21	*mast*	drunk
21	**Paghman**	a city near Kabul
21	**contrite**	apologetic and seeking forgiveness
21	**Kandahar**	the second largest city in Afghanistan, situated in the south
22	**Agha sahib**	a term of respect, like 'sir'
22	*Kochi*	Afghan nomads
23	*bazarris*	people who browse the stalls in bazaars
23	**Afghanis**	Afghan currency
26	**Chaman**	a town in Pakistan on the border with Afghanistan
27	*Kaka*	a term of familial affection, like 'uncle'
29	*Mashallah*	a quick prayer of thanks to God for an accomplishment
29	*Inshallah*	a phrase translating as 'God willing', expressing hope for a future event

CHAPTER 5

- The king of Afghanistan is overthrown in a coup.
- Amir and Hassan are attacked by three bullies – Assef, Wali and Kamal – but Hassan scares them off with his slingshot.
- Baba arranges for Hassan's cleft lip to be corrected as a birthday present.

CHECK THE POEM

Amir's description of the sound of the coup with its 'rapid staccato of gunfire' (p. 31) is reminiscent of a line from Wilfred Owen's war poem 'Anthem for Doomed Youth' (1917) where he describes 'the stuttering rifle's rapid rattle' (line 3).

CONTEXT

The coup which Amir describes occurred on 17 July 1973 when forces led by former Prime Minister Mohammed Daoud Khan overthrew the rule of King Zahir Shah. This saw the end of monarchy in Afghanistan.

The conversation between Amir and Hassan is interrupted by a loud roaring noise and the sound of gunfire. The boys, frightened, run to Ali who claims the noise was men hunting ducks. Ali hugs Hassan, making Amir jealous of this show of affection. This noise signalled the beginning of the end of what had been a sustained period of peace in Afghanistan. Baba returns in the morning having been delayed by roadblocks, and he hugs Amir, making him feel perversely happy about the frightening events of the previous night.

The explosions and gunfire had been the sounds of a coup overthrowing the king, Zahir Shah. Amir and Hassan listen to the news on the radio, and Hassan worries that the news means that he and his father will be sent away. He then suggests that they go and climb their tree, pleasing Amir by distracting him from the disturbing news. As they head towards the hill on which their tree grows Hassan is hit on the head by a stone. It has been thrown by a boy called Assef who approaches with his friends, Wali and Kamal. Assef is a notorious bully who carries steel knuckles to make his punches more damaging. The three approach Amir and Hassan, and Assef taunts Hassan and proclaims the coup as a good thing and expresses praise for Hitler. He declares that Afghanistan should be a Pashtun-only country.

As Assef starts to threaten Hassan, Amir asks him to let them go. Assef asks how Amir can have a Hazara as a friend. Amir almost protests that Hassan is not his friend but his servant. Assef dons his steel knuckles and makes to attack Amir, but Hassan threatens the bullies with a rock in a slingshot which he claims will remove one of Assef's eyes. The threat works and Assef and his friends leave, but only after Assef has promised his revenge on Hassan.

One result of the coup is talk of economic development and reform and life goes on in much the same way as before. Later, in the winter of 1974, on Hassan's birthday, the two boys are called in from playing for Hassan to receive his present from Baba. The present is Dr Kumar, a plastic surgeon, who has been brought in to correct Hassan's cleft lip. The surgery goes well and Hassan is left with no more than a faint scar. On emerging from the surgery, despite the swelling, Hassan attempts to smile. Amir informs us, however, in his role as **narrator**, that this was the winter when Hassan stopped smiling.

COMMENTARY

The disturbing noises of the coup are a sign of things changing in Amir's life and, in many different ways, can be seen as the true start of Amir's story with the previous chapters performing the function of introducing the characters and setting the scene. This is the chapter in which the conscious voice of the adult Amir recedes into the background of the story being told. The constant commenting and foregrounding falls away and it proceeds with a single **narrative** in the somewhat child-like tones of Amir's younger self.

This is also the chapter in which the traditional Afghanistan of which Amir has been talking starts to change into the modern war-torn country with which we, as readers, are more familiar. Amir comments as the gunfire and explosions sound outside their house: 'They were foreign sounds to us then. ... Huddled together in the dining room ... none of us had any notion that a way of life had ended' (pp. 31–2). The sounds of the coup are the start of the process which will lead to three decades of war.

Here too Amir's relationship with Hassan starts to change thanks to the bullying of Assef and his friends. They represent the first real outside threat to Amir's previously comfortable life. Assef introduces himself with an insult containing a sexual swear-word and Amir comments on his previous use of a different word, with similar connotations, as another term of abuse (p. 34). This creates a feeling of sexual threat which always accompanies Assef's role in the novel and **foreshadows** events to come.

CHECK THE BOOK

Hassan preventing the attack of Assef and his friends with his slingshot is reminiscent of the story of David using a slingshot to defeat the mighty Goliath in the book of Samuel in the Bible. This is a story which also appears in the Koran.

CHECK THE POEM

The **image** of a country on the verge of changing forever is also captured in Philip Larkin's poem 'MCMXIV' (1914), which evokes the last moments of pre-First World War Britain.

The fact that Amir allows Hassan to stand up for him simply reinforces the impression given in the earlier chapters of Amir's lack of self-confidence and of traditional 'macho' characteristics. It also opens up the gap between Amir and Hassan with Amir's thought, '*he's not my friend! ... He's my servant!*' (p. 36), showing how willing he is to sacrifice his friend for his own good.

Assef's mentioning of Hitler in admiring tones gives us extra information about how the ruling Pashtun class might view the Hazara people, and also an insight into the extreme character of this bully whom Amir refers to as a 'sociopath' (p. 34). He is representative of the violent, uncaring and self-destructive country which Afghanistan is in the process of becoming at this time.

By correcting Hassan's cleft lip, Baba reinforces his display of love for the boy and also once more provokes Amir's jealousy. It is a **symbol** of healing and restitution but this is overshadowed by Amir's final comment that the smile that Hassan attempts with his healing lip will be one of his last. Again, this statement **foreshadows** future events and warns readers that events are about to take a dark turn.

CONTEXT

Hitler and the Nazi regime aimed to rid the world of the Jewish people in what was known as the 'final solution'.

GLOSSARY

31	**staccato**	a musical term for notes which are short in duration and separated from each other
32	**republic**	a system of government with an elected or appointed president rather than an hereditary monarch
33	**brass knuckles**	a hand-held weapon cast of metal with holes for the fingers, used to reinforce the power of a punch
34	**sociopath**	a term for an antisocial personality disorder whereby the sufferer displays chronic immoral and antisocial behaviour
34	*kunis*	a term of abuse
36	*quwat*	bravery or conviction
36	*kasseef*	filthy
37	**hierarchy**	a system of levels from greatest to least
38	**constitutional monarchy**	a system of government based on the rule of a monarch
39	*Salaam alaykum*	traditional Arabic greeting meaning 'Peace be upon you'
40	**circumcision**	surgical removal of the foreskin

CHAPTER 6

- In winter the schools close and the children take part in kite-fighting tournaments.
- Hassan is a gifted kite runner.
- Amir tests Hassan's loyalty by asking him if he would eat dirt if commanded to do so.

Winter in Amir's childhood is the time when school is shut because of the ice, and the time when kite fighting takes place. Kites and kite fighting are the one thing which bring Amir and Baba together. In earlier years, Amir and Hassan would build their own kites and make their own *tar* (a kite string coated in ground glass), slicing their hands in the process. However, these kites were never very good. The boys were better at kite fighting than kite making, so Baba started to buy them kites from the best kite maker in the town, Saifo. If Amir asked for a larger, 'fancier kite' (p. 45), Baba would buy it for him, but then would buy the same for Hassan, making Amir wish he could be the favourite.

During kite fighting, when a string has been cut and the defeated kite flies away, the kite runners chase the kite trying to capture it when it lands and bring it home as a trophy. The last fallen kite of the winter tournament is the ultimate prize. Hassan, Amir explains, is the best kite runner, able to predict the path of a kite without having to watch it, positioning himself at the place where the kite will land before it gets there. One time Amir asks him how he does this and Hassan claims simply to know. Amir accuses him of lying and Hassan counters that he would sooner eat dirt than lie to Amir. Amir in return asks Hassan if he would really eat dirt if he was told to. Hassan looks strangely at Amir and affirms that he would. In return he asks if Amir would ever ask him to do so.

The winter of 1975 sees Hassan run his last kite. The tournament that year is to be held in Amir's neighbourhood and Baba suggests that perhaps Amir is now good enough to win. In return, Amir determines to do just that and make his father proud. The night before the tournament Hassan also suggests that Amir might win

QUESTION
Kite flying, kite fighting and kite running are all topics which recur throughout the novel. In what ways are these activities used not only to advance the plot but as **metaphors** for childhood, freedom, war and loss?

CHECK THE BOOK
The way Amir starts to mistreat Hassan, and his associated sense of guilt, is similar to how, in Dickens's *Great Expectations*, Pip's relationship with his brother-in-law, Joe, changes after he is informed of his new-found status as a gentleman. Hassan's tolerance and acceptance is also similar to Joe's.

the tournament. They are playing cards as they talk and Amir has a feeling that Hassan is letting him win.

COMMENTARY

Kite fighting is an activity which Amir and Hassan both enjoy and one in which they both excel, each with their own strengths: Amir at the fighting, Hassan at the running. As such it brings the two boys together more firmly than any of their other activities and bridges the gulf which Amir sometimes feels between them. It is also an activity of which his father approves and therefore provides Amir with a way to secure his father's love and admiration, describing it vividly as 'one paper-thin slice of intersection' (p. 43) between his and his father's otherwise separate spheres.

Kite flying is shown as a **symbol** of freedom and of independence. The idea of one kite against many is portrayed as typical of Afghan attitudes. In addition Amir admits that the glass-coated lines would cut his hands but he wouldn't mind. In other situations Amir avoids getting hurt or injured, but this fact shows that for something he truly believes in he is willing to risk himself.

Amir's descriptions of wintertime in Kabul reinforce this feeling of freedom as he uses poetic **imagery** to describe the city of his childhood. He says, 'The sky is seamless and blue, the snow so white my eyes burn' (p. 42), and later describes 'the soft pattering of snow against my window at night' and 'the way fresh snow crunched under my black rubber boots' (p. 43). By using such language he is able to convey the remembered love he feels for his home city and the beauty which it could achieve in this season.

The conversation between Amir and Hassan about Hassan eating dirt is another sign of the rift that Amir feels between himself and the other boy. It is also suggestive of an unease he seems to feel in placing himself in a superior situation to another human being. He is unsure how to handle this level of power and its responsibilities. Hassan's response, asking 'Would you ever ask me to do such a thing, Amir agha?' (p. 48), shows that he has a clearer understanding of the balance of power between the two of them than Amir does. This is reinforced when Hassan allows Amir to win at cards.

CHECK THE POEM

In 'Kite Poem' (2003), Joyce Carol Oates examines both the thrill and fear of kite flying. It seems an appropriate **metaphor** for Amir's dreams and the fears which hold him back.

CHECK THE POEM

A lively poem describing the joys of winter is Christina Rossetti's 'Winter: My Secret' (1862).

more glorious event, but makes the rape in the alley all the more dark and disturbing. It is as if the event has dirtied the clean, snow-white day.

GLOSSARY

54	**austere**	stern and cold, morally strict
54	**morose**	overly sad
54	*chapan*	a warm coat or cape worn over the clothes
55	*ayat*	a verse from the Koran
55	*diniyatclass*	religion class at school
63	*Bakhshida*	forgiven
67	**demise**	death, ending

CHAPTER 8

- After the events following the tournament, Amir feels guilty for not having helped Hassan.
- Hassan tries to patch up his relationship with Amir, but Amir rejects him.
- Amir has a birthday and Assef the bully comes to the party and brings him a biography of Hitler as a present.

For the week after the tournament Amir hardly sees his friend. Normal chores are carried out, but Hassan retreats to his bed afterwards. Ali asks Amir if something had happened, but Amir denies any knowledge of any violence and suggests Hassan is simply sick.

That night Amir asks his father to take him to Jalalabad at the weekend. Baba suggests they ask Hassan, but Amir informs him he is ill and they determine to go without him. However, rather than just the two of them, Baba invites a range of relatives and friends and three vans full of people leave for Jalalabad. On the journey Baba proudly boasts about Amir winning the tournament, but Amir is unable to join in as he is feeling car sick. He asks them to pull over but they don't manage in time and he is sick in the van. As he recovers, with his eyes shut, behind his eyes all he can see are Hassan's trousers discarded in the alley.

GLOSSARY

42	*qurma*	stew
49	**viable**	capable of surviving/succeeding
50	*panjpar*	a card game

CHAPTER 7

- Amir wins the kite-fighting tournament and Hassan runs to catch his kite.
- Hassan is captured by Assef and the other bullies in an alley. He is raped.
- Amir sees the attack on Hassan but does nothing to help him.

On the morning of the tournament Hassan recounts to Amir a dream he has had the night before in which the two boys swim out into a lake which is supposed to contain a monster lurking beneath the surface. The people on the bank are so impressed with their bravery, and pleased to find there is no monster, that they rename the lake after the two boys. Neither one knows what the dream might mean.

The two boys leave for the tournament and Amir is nervous, wishing to back out. Hassan encourages him and, recalling his dream, comforts him, saying there is no monster. Amir flies his kite and while other kites are being cut, he maintains its intact. He sees Baba and Rahim Khan watching from the roof of the house and hopes his father is cheering for him. Amir keeps his kite in the sky until his is one of the last two kites remaining. He feels the blossoming of the knowledge that he is going to win and shortly after takes advantage of a gust to cut his opponent's line. He has won. Hassan leaves to run after the defeated blue kite for his master.

Amir returns home to congratulations from Ali. He gives him his kite and returns to the streets to await Hassan with his prize of the defeated kite. He searches for Hassan. An old man wants to know why Amir is looking for Hassan and is scathing about Hazaras, but points Amir in Hassan's direction. He also says that the servant was being chased.

CONTEXT

The reporting of dreams is a common technique used in literature. It can be used as a way of revealing hidden knowledge that characters cannot see for themselves. This is an idea examined by the Swiss psychiatrist Carl Jung (1875–1961) in his work on dream interpretation, asserting that dreams are the way the unconscious mind communicates with the conscious one.

Amir hurries after Hassan, continuing his search, and finally hears voices in an alley. He looks in and sees Hassan standing in a defensive posture in front of the kite he has claimed for his master. Between Amir and Hassan are the three bullies – Assef, Wali and Kamal.

Assef offers to let Hassan go free if he will give up the blue kite. Hassan refuses, asserting that the kite is the property of Amir. He picks up a rock and threatens the bullies, but he does not have his slingshot with him. Assef allows Hassan to keep the kite as a reminder of what is about to happen, and then he attacks. Amir watches, unseen by the bullies, unable and unwilling to bring himself to say anything to stop the attack.

The story is interrupted by two memories and a dream illustrating Amir's relationship with Hassan: their tight brotherhood and the barrier between them. Amir continues his story with Hassan having been overwhelmed by the three bullies; they have stripped him of his trousers. Assef is preparing to rape Hassan. Amir sees the look on Hassan's face and recognises it as the same look of resignation he had on his face when Amir asked him if he would eat dirt for him.

Another memory intervenes, a memory of the ritual slaughter of a sheep before the celebration of a Muslim ceremony. Amir is haunted by the look of acceptance in the sheep's eyes. This is the same look he identifies in Hassan's eyes. Amir turns away from the alley, unable to witness the awful thing happening to Hassan. He has bitten his fist to keep from crying out and his hand is bleeding. He turns and runs away. He waits in the bazaar as first the bullies run past, and then Hassan arrives. During his wait he analyses his feelings of guilt. When Hassan arrives, Amir wonders if he knows that Amir saw what happened. Hassan is very shaken and clearly in pain, but nothing is said. Amir takes the kite from him and they return home. The welcome from his father is exactly what Amir had wanted for so long. Enfolded in his father's arms he forgets his cowardice.

COMMENTARY

This is the key chapter of the novel and provides the event on which the rest of the story hangs. The rape of Hassan by Assef is the event that Amir has been **foreshadowing** in earlier chapters and one

CHECK THE BOOK

Ian McEwan's *Atonement* (2001) is another novel where the central theme is based on the witnessing of a sexual attack and the lasting effect it has on those involved.

which he refers back to in future chapters. It opens with Hassan talking about his dream. In it he and Amir are acclaimed as heroes. With this being the chapter featuring the kite-fighting tournament this would seem to be a positive omen for the coming competition. It also demonstrates Hassan's positive state of mind and again reinforces his allegiance for and love of Amir. However, with the image of the lurking monster 'swimming at the bottom, waiting' (p. 52), there is a suggestion that Hassan is conscious of the cruelty which hides beneath Amir's friendly surface and wishes his friend to banish this side of his personality, just as he banishes the monster in the dream.

The **juxtaposition** of the tournament and the attack means that the act of winning is immediately contrasted with the act of losing, and the latter is shown to outweigh the former. Upon witnessing the rape Amir is forced to choose between his friend and his father, and by not acting he chooses his father.

At the moment just before the rape, Amir sees Hassan's expression and recognises it as the same look of resignation that the boy wore when Amir was asking him if he would eat dirt if ordered to. In this way Amir draws a direct comparison between what he threatened to do to Hassan and what Assef is actually doing, making him almost as bad as the bully. During the rape, Amir's **narrative** breaks off to talk about memories rather than the events actually occurring. This shows the **narrator**'s difficulty in dealing with this part of the story directly, but also the way his mind, as a boy, may have tried to distance himself from what he was seeing.

The fact that the rape occurs in an alley is significant. It is not a main street, it is dark, and rarely used, representing the illicit and secret nature of the act. Amir's viewing of the attack is akin to sexual voyeurism and so makes admitting to the event all the harder because of the connotations of seeing something he shouldn't have been looking at. It also makes it possible for him to dismiss the event because it did not happen in the mainstream of life, but as an aside.

All these events occur on a clear winter's day with the sun shining from a clear blue sky, which Amir refers to before the rape as 'blameless' (p. 53). This makes the winning of the tournament a

CONTEX

Motion s
such as t
suffered
usually c
differenc
percepti
between
amount
moveme
detected
eyes and
ear. This
leads to
and vom
There ar
many tre
for it. Ho
Amir's si
probably
some for
anxiety a
rather th
motion s

Amir is not as happy in Jalalabad as he expected. He lies awake after everyone else is asleep and remembers Hassan's dream. He concludes there was a monster in the lake after all – and it was him. The following week Hassan and Amir speak again. Hassan invites Amir to climb the hill to their tree. They do so but, once there, Amir wants to return to his room. They walk back in silence.

Over the winter Amir tries to keep his relationship with his father at the same high level of affection, but when his father is out of the house he hides away with his books. Hassan keeps trying to make peace with his master, but Amir doesn't want to. He is mean to Hassan in the hope that the other boy will retaliate. After that, Amir does his best to stay out of Hassan's way. One day Amir asks his father about the possibility of getting new servants. His father is angered by the idea and expresses his love for Ali and Hassan.

With the return to school, Amir is able to forget about Hassan to some extent, but one afternoon he invites him to accompany him up the hill to the pomegranate tree. Once there he throws pomegranates at Hassan and tries to get him to fight back. Hassan refuses no matter how much Amir shouts at him until finally he picks up a pomegranate and crushes it on his own forehead in an effort to please his master. Amir holds Hassan and cries.

By the summer Amir's relationship with Baba has cooled again. Despite this, his father throws a large birthday party for his son and invites a host of guests, most of whom Amir doesn't know. However, one group of guests comprises the bully Assef and his family. Assef is flattering towards Baba, but Amir senses that there is a tension between the boy and his parents, and that maybe they are afraid of their own child. Baba seems vaguely embarrassed by his son in the face of Assef's more assertive and manly ways. Amir takes the present from Assef and leaves the party to find somewhere quiet to open it. It is a biography of Hitler. He throws it away. He stays sitting in the patch of wasteland he has found until Rahim Khan finds him. The man relates a story of the servant girl he wished to marry and how the rest of his family prevented it. His moral is that the world always triumphs over personal wishes. He informs Amir that he can confide anything in him and Amir almost does, but backs down at the last minute. Rahim Khan then gives

> **CONTEXT**
>
> According to the Koran pomegranates are one of the fruits that Muslims will find in the garden of paradise; they are supposed to be a cure for envy and hatred.

CHECK THE BOOK

Rahim Khan's story about the Hazara girl he fell in love with is similar to the story of Shakespeare's *Romeo and Juliet* with its tale of doomed and forbidden love.

CONTEXT

Hassan's refusal to fight back when Amir attacks him with the pomegranates would seem to be similar to the Christian idea of 'turning the other cheek' expressed in Matthew 5.38–41. However, the theme of acceptance without retribution is common to most religions including Islam. The thirty-second of the Forty Hadith of an-Nawawi, which gathers together the sayings of the prophet, is: 'There should be neither harming nor reciprocating harm.'

Amir his birthday present from him, a leather-bound notebook to write his stories in. As Amir takes the present fireworks start to explode in the sky and in the flashes of light he sees Hassan serving drinks to Assef and another of the bullies. In a second flash he sees Assef bullying Hassan.

COMMENTARY

In the aftermath of the rape Amir tries to pretend the events have not occurred. He denies knowing anything, avoids Hassan and convinces Baba to take him away from the house without bringing Hassan, literally distancing himself from his problems. Amir's later request that his father get rid of the servants is a further example of him trying to distance himself from his guilt, this time by removing them from his home. The car sickness and insomnia he suffers from are other signs of his weakness demonstrated to Baba. With no outward expression, Amir's guilt has become something physical.

Amir's realisation that he was the monster in Hassan's dream has a self-pitying and melodramatic tone to it as he tells us 'he'd been wrong about that. There was a monster in the lake. ... I was that monster' (p. 75). Thus we start to see how Amir views his guilt and illness as a deserved punishment for his lack of ability to help Hassan, just as his poor relationship with his father is his punishment for his having 'killed' his mother during his birth.

Amir's and Hassan's return to their usual spot under the pomegranate tree is significant: this location is no longer the refuge from the world it used to be because Amir still brings his feelings of guilt with him. In a replay of the 'eating dirt' scene, which has already been compared in Amir's mind to the moment of rape, Amir attacks Hassan with the pomegranates which used to be a **symbol** of their bond, thus finalising the breaking of the bond. By reacting as he does, hitting himself with a final pomegranate, Hassan once more shows the acceptance which Amir saw on his face at the time of the rape and refuses to let Amir assuage his guilt by fighting back against him.

The presence of Assef and his family at the birthday party creates a feeling of a shadow falling across the occasion. The spectre of Hitler is once more raised in Assef's gift. By giving this book to Amir, a symbolic link is made again between Assef's bullying and Amir's refusal to help. The final vision is of Assef bullying Hassan at the party and Amir once more unable to bring himself to stop it, reinforcing this idea.

GLOSSARY

72	*Khala* a familiar term of affection, similar to 'Aunt'
74	**lamb kabob** spiced lamb often cooked on a stick
74	*tandoor* a clay oven
75	**insomniac** a person who is unable to sleep
86	*pari* fairy or angel

CHAPTER 9

- Hassan and Ali give Amir a birthday present of a copy of the book Amir used to read to Hassan.
- Amir falsely accuses Hassan of stealing birthday presents.
- Ali and Hassan leave Baba's service.

The day after his birthday party, Amir opens all his presents but is unable to raise any enthusiasm for them, even the bicycle and the expensive watch his father has bought for him. One exception is a notebook he receives from Rahim Khan. Amir finally takes his bicycle out for a ride and passes by the hut in which Ali and Hassan live. Ali gives him a birthday present from the two of them, a new copy of the storybook from which Amir used to read to Hassan. The gift of the book raises a lump in Amir's throat, but he still adds it to the pile of other discarded presents. Before retiring to bed he asks his father if he has seen his new watch anywhere.

The next morning Amir waits for Ali and Hassan to leave their hut before planting his watch and some money under Hassan's mattress. He then goes to his father and lies to him about the servants. Following their discussion, Baba talks to Ali and then comes back to call Amir to a meeting with Ali, Hassan and himself.

 CHECK THE POEM

The concept of gifts or earnings being tainted by the actions of the receiver, as expressed by the term 'blood money' (p. 89), refers back to the pieces of silver paid to Judas Iscariot for betraying Jesus. This image is used by Walt Whitman in his 1850 poem attacking a fugitive-slave law, entitled 'Blood Money'.

Ali and Hassan stand before Baba and Amir. The two servants have been crying. Baba asks Hassan if he stole the money and watch; he admits it. Amir flinches at this response but then realises this is another sacrifice like the ones Hassan has been making for him all his life. In that moment Amir realises that Hassan knows that Amir saw the events in the alley and that Hassan is once more taking the blame in order to save his master. Baba then surprises Amir by forgiving Hassan, despite his having previously said that theft is the worst sin. However, Ali announces that it is impossible to stay and that he and Hassan are leaving. Amir realises that Hassan has told Ali all that has happened and feels relieved and then ashamed. Baba tries to convince Ali to stay, but he refuses and explains that they are going to Hazarajat to stay with his cousin. In response, Baba cries and pleads, something which Amir has never seen him do before.

It is raining as Ali and Hassan climb into Baba's car to go to the bus station. Amir imagines the scene as if from a Hindi movie. He imagines running through the rain after the car and catching it up. He and Hassan would hug and all would be forgiveness. However, this is only imagination. He simply watches as the car drives away.

COMMENTARY

Amir opens his presents but, as with the time he spends alone with his father in the previous chapter and even his possession of the kite at the end of the tournament, he takes no pleasure in them. His guilt over what happened to Hassan, and his failure to do anything to help, overshadow any joy he might get from the gifts. He sees them as the profits of his sins rather than as a reward for doing well in the tournament and as such does not feel he deserves them. The concept that he invokes of them being 'blood money' (p. 89) is reflected most keenly in the fact that the bike his father gives him is a rich red colour.

There are only two presents which mean anything to him. The notebook Rahim Khan gives him is a reward for his writing rather than his kite flying and so is not sullied by the events of Hassan's rape. It is also **symbolic** of the one ability which makes Amir an individual, his ability to write. The second significant present, the storybook chosen by Hassan, also has these connections but it acts as a reminder of what he has lost by his cowardly actions. This provokes Amir's guilt and converts it into action, leading to his subsequent framing of Hassan for the theft of his other presents.

Where the pomegranate attack was a straightforward attempt by Amir to relieve his guilt by allowing Hassan to take revenge on him, Amir's planting of his supposedly 'stolen' birthday presents under Hassan's mattress is an attempt to remove his guilt by removing its cause. It is also the next step in his attempt to put distance between himself and Hassan. This time he is successful, but the fact of Ali and Hassan leaving makes Amir finally realise that he should have been honest about what he saw. He imagines how, in a film, he would 'chase the car, screaming for it to stop ... pull Hassan out of the backseat and tell him [he] was sorry, so sorry' (p. 94). However, this realisation comes too late and Amir is left with his guilty secret. Once Hassan has taken the blame, Baba forgives him, once more demonstrating a remarkable level of affection for his servant's son.

The other key moment in this scene is Amir's realisation that Ali finally knows what has happened to his son and Amir's role in the affair. However, he reflects the attitude of his son and does not say anything to Baba, protecting Amir but also refusing to relieve him of his guilt. Ali and Hassan leaving causes Baba to cry, something which we would not expect from the character already presented to us. This is then reflected in another moment of **pathetic fallacy** in the rain storm which accompanies their departure. Amir tells us that summer rain was rare, just as his father's tears were rare. Amir himself does not cry, but the rain instead provides symbolic tears for him to view the departure through.

CONTEXT

The gift from Hassan of a new copy of the *Shahnamah* is not merely symbolic of the boy's friendship. The title of the book translates as 'The Book of Kings' and recalls Amir's carving of 'Amir and Hassan, the sultans of Kabul' (p. 24) into the pomegranate tree, as well as Hassan's remembrance of the phrase in his dream before the kite-fighting tournament, bonding them firmly together.

GLOSSARY

88 **Polaroid** a camera which takes photos which develop instantly

88 **transistor radio** a small portable radio

93 **rickshaws** small carts for carrying people usually pulled by other people

94 *raka'ts* the sections of the ritual Islamic prayers

CHAPTER 10

- It is 1981 and Amir and his father are escaping from Russian-controlled Afghanistan.
- Baba stands up to a Russian soldier who wishes to rape a female Afghan refugee.
- One of the bullies from the attack in the alley, Kamal, who is also escaping, dies on the journey.

The story moves to March 1981. Amir and his father are cramped together with a dozen strangers in the back of an old Russian truck. They are leaving Kabul, escaping Afghanistan. Amir is once more hit by car sickness and Baba is again forced to apologise for his son's weakness. The truck stops so that Amir can be sick and while he stands by the roadside he thinks of the house they have left behind. They have abandoned everything as if merely leaving for the day, hoping to prevent anyone from realising that they have left for good and therefore prevent pursuit by occupying Russian forces.

The journey continues and they are stopped at a Russian roadblock. The driver pays the guards a bribe but one of them wants half an hour with one of the female passengers. Baba stands up and confronts the Russian, protecting the woman and daring the guard to shoot him. Amir tries to get his father to sit down, but his father slaps his hand away, complaining of his son's cowardice and promising to kill the guard if he is not felled by the man's first bullet. There is a gunshot and Amir believes his father to have been shot, but it is a Russian officer who has fired a warning shot into the air to calm the guard. The officer lets the truck pass and as they continue the young woman's husband moves over and kisses Baba's hand.

They arrive in Jalalabad only to find that the truck they have been promised will take them out of Afghanistan is broken. Karim, who has brought them this far, says that it happened the week before. Baba starts to throttle Karim because he realises that the man has brought them this far purely to get his own cut of the money they are paying for their escape, but now they have no chance of actually completing their journey. Baba stops choking him only when the young woman from the truck begs him to stop. Then they hear

CONTEXT

The Soviet army entered Afghanistan in 1979 to oppose groups of Afghan Mujahedin rebels and started a war which lasted until the Soviets finally withdrew in 1989. Many Afghans fled the country and found sanctuary in places like Pakistan and, due to the anti-Soviet sentiments of the Cold War, the USA.

banging from the basement of the house. It is the noise of other people who have been brought here under similar false pretences. They have been waiting two weeks. Karim has no answer to Baba's question of when the truck might be fixed.

They go down to wait, hidden in the basement with the others, and Karim informs them it will be only a couple of days before the truck is repaired. They live in the basement for a week. Amir discovers that the other people in the basement include the bully, Kamal, and his father. Kamal looks awful and Amir overhears Kamal's father telling Baba that Kamal has been raped by a number of men.

After a week Karim finally informs them that the truck will not be mended but that they can be smuggled in in a fuel tanker. Once in the tanker Amir starts to panic and is unable to breathe in the stinking dark. Baba calms him by showing him the light from his wristwatch and encouraging him to think of something good. He thinks of a day spent flying a kite with Hassan. They finally reach Pakistan and emerge from the tanker. As Amir recovers from the journey he hears Kamal's father wailing. His son has died during the journey in the tanker. Kamal's father stands and lunges for Karim. He grabs the man's gun, places it in his mouth, and kills himself.

COMMENTARY

The action moves abruptly forward in time by five years from the moment of the departure of Ali and Hassan to the flight of Baba and Amir from Afghanistan. Amir is now eighteen years old. By this time the country was occupied by Russian troops and many people chose to emigrate and leave everything behind rather than continue to live in what had become a very dangerous country.

Amir is struck with car sickness during their escape, once more revealing his weakness in front of his father and embarrassing him. This is contrasted with the scene of Baba showing his strength and bravery by preventing the Russian soldier from raping the woman in the truck. This moment also acts as a contrast with Amir's actions in the alley where he did not prevent the rape of Hassan.

CHECK THE FILM

The 2007 film *Charlie Wilson's War*, starring Tom Hanks, examines the way in which the US government funded the Mujahedin rebels in the war against the Soviet and Afghan communists.

CONTEXT

'Ahesta Bero', the song which the Russian soldier is singing as he contemplates his rape of the Afghan refugee, is the song sung at Afghan, Iranian and Tajik weddings to accompany the entrance of the bride and groom, similar to Richard Wagner's 'Bridal Chorus' (often called 'The Wedding March') which is used in Christian ceremonies.

CHECK THE POEM

The Khyber Pass through which Amir and his father pass to reach Pakistan has long been identified as a natural border between Russian-held lands and the Indian sub-continent, as in Rudyard Kipling's poem, 'The Ballad of the King's Jest' (1890).

The Russian soldier who wishes to rape the woman is singing an Afghan wedding song as he approaches the truck. This shows how much the Russians have become part of Afghan life, but also how little respect they have for the Afghans themselves that he should sing such a song and then attempt such an action.

After Baba saves the woman from rape, her husband kneels and kisses Baba's hand. This demonstrates, as with Amir's previous tales of his father, the regard that other Afghans have for Baba, regardless of the circumstances. It also shows a culture of respect that is absent from the driver of the truck who has taken their money to pay for the escape. In these two actions we see the traditional Afghanistan, where there is a spirit of community and mutual respect, and the new Afghanistan, which is a land of unrest, exploitation and personal struggle.

There is a vivid description of the basement in which Amir and his father wait for the final part of their journey. Amir describes how he can see 'shapes huddled around the room, their silhouettes thrown on the walls by the dim light of a pair of kerosene lamps', and later, 'I discovered the source of the scratching sounds. Rats' (p. 104). In this short passage a claustrophobic environment is laid out in stark contrast to Amir's earlier descriptions of the house Baba built for them. It demonstrates the change in their status which their flight from Afghanistan has caused. This is extended in the change into the present tense for the description of the interior of the oil tanker in which they make the final leg of the journey.

Despite its initial horror, the death of Kamal on the escape from Afghanistan can be seen as **symbolic** of a chance for Amir to escape his problems and the potential for him to move on with his life in a new country, without bringing all of the 'baggage' of his past with him.

GLOSSARY		
97	*Shorawi*	Soviets
97	**Peshawar**	large city in northern Pakistan
98	*rafiqs*	companions
98	**Poleh-charkhi**	Afghan prison
98	**Kalashnikov**	a Russian rifle
99	**MiG**	Russian fighter-plane

99	*Spasseba*	Russian for 'thank you'
100	**negate**	cancel out
101	*Roussi*	Russians
107	*rubab*	a stringed instrument similar to a guitar
107	**encapsulated**	expressed in brief terms, summed up

CHAPTER 11

- It is the 1980s and Amir and Baba are now living in the USA.
- Baba is a little unsettled there but is still capable of commanding respect.
- Baba and Amir buy items from garage sales and sell them from a stall in the Afghan section of the San Jose flea market.
- Amir falls in love with a girl named Soraya whom he meets at the flea market.

The story moves on once again, now to Fremont, California, in the 1980s. Amir relates how much his father loves America but, how, at the same time it is the cause of his ulcer. He likes the idea of America as it seems to represent strength. He likes Ronald Regan and is the only Republican supporter in their building. However, the air and water pollution and lack of fresh foods make him ill. He also refuses to improve his English and finds it hard to accept some of the customs of his new country.

Baba loses his temper in a shop when asked for identification to accompany a cheque. His pride will not let him accept that this is normal rather than a slur on his character. Baba misses his homeland. Amir, in contrast, embraces America as a way of forgetting his past. He suggests returning to Pakistan but Baba will not because America is better for Amir. Baba has found a job only one month after arriving in the USA and has handed back his food-stamps on the same day, rejecting charity and maintaining his self-respect.

In 1983, Amir graduates from high school at the age of twenty and afterwards his father tells him he is proud of him. He then takes

CONTEXT

The parts of the novel set in and around San Jose and San Francisco reflect Khaled Hosseini's own life. Having left Afghanistan, his family settled in San Jose in 1980, and it was here that Hosseini attended high school, college and medical school.

CONTEXT

Baba's graduation present to Amir is a Ford Gran Torino (mis-named a 'Grand Torino' in the novel). This was the car made famous in the television action series *Starsky and Hutch*. It is a reminder of the Ford Mustang Baba owned in Kabul, which was the car driven by Steve McQueen in the 1968 film *Bullitt*. This ties in with Amir's love of American films and culture.

CHECK THE BOOK

The central section of *The Kite Runner* is set in an Afghan community in California. In this it is similar to other **post-colonial** novels such as Zadie Smith's *White Teeth* (2000) and Monica Ali's *Brick Lane* (2003), which chart the experiences of Bangladeshi immigrants and their children living in contemporary London.

Amir to a bar and proceeds to get drunk. By the time they leave, everyone in the bar is sorry to see Baba leave. On their return home, Baba gives Amir a graduation present of a car. As they sit in the car and Amir thanks his father, Baba wishes Hassan could be with them and Amir suffers a panic attack. Following high school Amir decides to study English and Creative Writing at college. His father wants him to study something which will lead to a 'proper job' but Amir stands his ground.

In 1984, Baba buys an old Volkswagen bus and he and Amir travel around, buying goods from garage and lawn sales before taking them to a stall at the San Jose flea market to sell. An entire section of the market is run by Afghans. Many of the people know each other and it is as though a small section of Afghanistan has been transplanted into America. One man whom Amir is introduced to by his father is General Taheri, who worked for the Ministry of Defence in Afghanistan. They talk and this influential man describes Baba as being a great man. The conversation is halted by the general's daughter, Soraya, arriving with a drink for her father. Amir sees her and is immediately attracted to her. He asks his father about her and discovers that there was once a man in her life but things ended badly and she has had no suitors since. However, lying in bed that night, all Amir can think about is her beautiful face. He is in love.

COMMENTARY

This chapter echoes the events of Chapter 3 in which Amir describes his father's reputation. Once again he outlines events which demonstrate Baba's pride and the stature which he has in his community. However, these are all now set in an American context and these attributes are seen slightly differently. Amir is seen to fit in better in America than his father, placating the grocery clerk and graduating from high school. However, Baba's natural ability to garner the respect of others is shown to be as potent in this new country when he becomes the new best friend of the customers in the bar where they go to celebrate Amir's graduation.

Baba's trading of small items in the San Jose market is also a reflection of the tale told in Chapter 3 of Baba becoming a successful merchant against the odds. Again it is in a new context, one in which Baba is a newly arrived immigrant, but it shows a continuation of the same spirit and also, from Amir's **narrative** of these events, that he still holds his father in the same regard. The desire to be part of the flea market in San Jose is also a way for Baba to hold onto his heritage. He trades within the Afghan part of the market; many of the others there are people he knew back in Afghanistan. As such he is able to retain a small piece of what he has left behind.

In this chapter Amir meets Soraya. She, like Amir, is the child of an influential, powerful and well-regarded man. She is also a beautiful young woman who makes an instant impression on Amir. Baba's comment on Soraya's past, that 'a few days, sometimes even a single day, can change the course of a whole lifetime' (pp. 123–4) is key here. It is a sentiment to which Amir can relate, and the suggestion is that it forms a significant part of his attraction to her.

> **CONTEXT**
>
> Soraya Taheri is one of the few female characters in the novel, and certainly the most prominent. She shares her name with a former queen of Afghanistan, the wife of King Amanullah Khan. She was an early and powerful champion of women's rights in Afghanistan.

> **GLOSSARY**
>
> 110 **Jimmy Carter** 39th president of the USA, 1977–81
> 110 **Leonid Brezhnev** Soviet premier, 1964–82
> 110 **Ronald Reagan** 40th president of the USA, 1981–9
> 110 **ESL** English as a second language
> 110 **Amtrak** American railway system
> 116 **Hayward** a city in California, near to San Francisco
> 117 *khanum* literally 'queen', a courteous title for a woman
> 117 *chatti* a term of derision

CHAPTER 12

- Amir is in love with Soraya, but is warned off by her father.
- Baba falls ill with lung cancer.
- Amir asks his father to approach Soraya's family for her hand in marriage, and it is all agreed.

Amir informs us that, as a child, Ali had told him that *yelda*, the first night of winter, was a night when animals and insects searched

CHECK THE POEM

The idea of keeping vigil is always a poignant one in literature whether it is the love-stricken wait of Romeo and Juliet or the vigil of death held on the battlefield in Walt Whitman's 'Vigil Strange I Kept on the Field One Night' (1865) in which a soldier watches over a fallen comrade's body, expressing his love for his fellow soldier.

CONTEXT

During the descriptions of Baba's illness, Amir provides us with all the technical language associated with the treatment of cancer. This largely replaces the use of Farsi and Pashtun words in earlier chapters, creating the impression that these medical terms are the hidden language of America, a country which is, at least for Baba, a place of sickness.

for the lost sun. When older, Amir learned that *yelda* was the night of lovers' vigils. After meeting Soraya, every weeknight becomes *yelda* with him waiting for the Sunday markets to see her again.

On Sundays, Amir walks through the market so that he can get glimpses of the girl. He finally decides to approach her. Baba warns Amir not to embarrass him, and to be mindful of the traditions of the girl's father. He waits until the general is absent and then approaches. He pretends to have been looking for the father, but then makes a direct enquiry to her. They talk about the book she is reading and his writings. He offers to let her read a story of his. As he is about to leave, Soraya's mother, Khala Jamila, appears and she is very pleased to see Amir, welcoming him.

This encounter forms the start of a pattern, with Amir talking to Soraya, and her mother, when the general is away from his stall. This continues until one day the general returns and speaks to Amir, reminding him that everyone in the market is watching and reporting back to him. This is his way of warning Amir away from his daughter. Amir does not get a chance to brood on this warning, because his father falls ill with a bad cough. This quickly becomes worse and an X-ray shows up a spot on one lung. After further tests it is diagnosed as lung cancer. Baba refuses chemotherapy as he is told it will only help, not cure. He also instructs Amir to let no one know about his illness.

They carry on at the flea markets, despite the cancer, but slowly Amir takes over the duties of haggling and selling. Finally, one day, Baba collapses at the market and is rushed to hospital. General Taheri and his family come to visit and some of the general's recent coolness seems to have disappeared. Two days later Baba is discharged and, once home, Amir asks him to approach the general for Soraya's hand in marriage. Baba agrees and calls the general on the phone to arrange a meeting. The next morning Baba drives off on his own to the meeting. Later Baba calls from the general's house to say that Amir's proposal has been accepted but that Soraya wishes to speak to him first. She explains to him that, when her family lived in Virginia, she ran away with an Afghan man and lived with him for a month. He is troubled by this, but tells Soraya that

he still wants to marry her. He compares the revelation of her secret
with the continued concealment of his own secret and wishes he
was as brave as her.

COMMENTARY

Amir opens the chapter as he ended the previous one, by describing
his feelings for Soraya. In both instances his use of descriptive
language comes to the fore once again. He talks about 'the shadow
her hair cast on the ground when it slid off her back and hung down
like a velvet curtain' (pp. 125–6) and calls her '[t]he morning sun to
my *yelda*' (p. 126). This recalls the poetic language he used when
introducing Hassan and discussing Kabul in winter. This style of
language is associated with the most fundamental things in Amir's
life, and shows the high level of regard in which he holds Soraya.

During one of their conversations, Soraya explains how she taught
the servant they had in their house back in Afghanistan to read. This
contrasts with Amir's refusal to teach Hassan and, in fact, with his
teasing of him for being illiterate and the way he would teach him
the wrong meanings of words he didn't know. Amir sees in Soraya
both echoes of his mother but also a reflection of the version of
himself that he wishes he could have been.

Soraya's mother is much more welcoming to Amir. This is not a sign
that she is any less a traditional Afghan than her husband but more
a sign of how desperate she is for any young man to pay attention to
her daughter, due to Soraya's history. Again, the fear that no one
will want her daughter because she has been with another man
stems from a traditional Afghan view of marriage. Amir's
willingness to overlook this fact is partly due to his Americanisation
but also his reluctance to condemn another for the sins in their past
because of the continuing weight of his guilt over Hassan.

In contrast to Amir's happiness at being in the USA, Baba has not
adapted so well. To that extent his illness can be seen as a reaction to
being there, or rather to not being in Afghanistan. There is an
element of pining in the way he wastes away. However, the host of
people who visit him in hospital is a sign that the regard of others
has not diminished.

CONTEXT

The San Jose flea
market claims to
be not only the
largest such
market in the USA,
but also in the
world. In existence
since 1960 it is
sited in the middle
of what is known
as Silicon Valley
(an area of
California
renowned for
manufacture of
computers,
software and other
technology reliant
on the silicon chip)
and covers 120
acres. It is famous
for selling a vast
range of goods.

CONTEXT

Khastegari (p. 141) is the formal ceremony for proposing marriage in Afghan and Iranian culture. Usually the suitor himself approaches the other family, accompanied by his parents, and asks politely for permission to marry their daughter. That Amir sends his father, without attending himself, shows both a respect for his father, but also another side to his timidity.

GLOSSARY

126 **ahmaq** fool

127 **mozahem** an intruder

127 **Khoda hafez** goodbye, literally 'God, safe'

128 **lochak** a swindler

128 **mohtaram** repected

130 **ahesta boro** Afghan bridal music

130 **henna** a paste used for temporary tattoos

131 **chaperoning** accompanying young unmarried people to ensure nothing improper occurs

133 **bachem** my child

134 **pulmonary** relating to the heart

135 **CAT scan** a medical scan which produces a 3-D image of the inside of the body-part scanned

136 **bronchoscopy** an examination procedure where a small camera is inserted into the airways

136 **prognosis** prediction of the course of an illness

136 **chemotherapy** treatment using chemicals, usually a term used when treating cancers

136 **palliative** treating of the symptoms rather than curing the disease

138 **Komak!** Help!

138 **911** emergency telephone number in the USA (999 in the UK)

139 **metastasized** spread

140 **oncologist** doctor specialising in cancer

141 **Balay** yes

CHAPTER 13

- Amir marries Soraya.
- Baba dies.
- Amir publishes his first novel.
- Amir and Soraya find that they are unable to have children.

The next day Amir and his father go to the Taheris' house for the official proposal. They arrive to find two dozen guests waiting for them. Baba is pleased that this is being done in the proper Afghan way. He makes the formal proposal and Soraya is finally summoned. She enters and sits next to Amir as all the guests applaud. Traditionally the engagement period should take place over a few months, but this is cut short because of Baba's ill health. The wedding is held in traditional fashion and reminds Amir of Kabul. He wishes Rahim Khan was there, and he wonders if Hassan has also married.

After they are married, Soraya suggests that she move in with Amir rather than find their own house, so that they can look after his sick father. Soraya dedicates herself to looking after Baba. One day Amir returns home to find Soraya hiding Amir's leather-bound notebook under Baba's blanket. His father has been reading his stories at last and is amazed by them. Amir leaves the room to cry.

A month after the wedding, Baba dies. At the funeral Amir remembers the great stature of his father in Kabul; the testimonials of his friends make him realise how much of himself is tied up with his image of his father. With Baba gone, Amir learns more about his new family. He discovers that the general suffers from bad migraines once a month and that he is still waiting for Afghanistan to be restored so that he can go back and resume his government work. He learns that, since a stroke years earlier, Khala Jamila is constantly concerned for her own health. But also she is relieved that someone has finally married her daughter: this translates into a great love for Amir.

Amir also learns more details of Soraya's earlier affair, of her father turning up at the man's house with two bullets in his gun, one for the man and one for himself. Amir does not worry about this part of her past and Soraya is surprised and happy about this, commenting that Amir is 'so different from every Afghan guy I've met' (p. 157). Amir surmises that his lack of anxiety about her past mistakes is because he has so many regrets of his own.

Amir and Soraya get their own apartment and Amir secures his place at college studying English. The following year Soraya also enrols, to study to be a teacher. In the summer of 1988, Amir finishes writing his first novel. He secures an agent and soon hears

CHECK THE BOOK

In *The Kabul Beauty School* (2007), Deborah Rodriguez describes having visited post-9/11 Afghanistan with the aim of connecting with the country's women. Among other topics she looks closely at the various intricacies of Afghan wedding ceremonies.

As Amir publishes his first book, the Soviet armies pull out of Afghanistan. This occurred in response to the collapse of the Soviet Union, the fall of the Berlin Wall and the end of the Cold War. However, rather than allowing the Afghans to re-establish peace, leaders of the militias established themselves as warlords with their own areas of control, and civil war continued.

CHECK THE POEM

Rumi, a thirteenth-century Persian poet listed as one of those Amir studied at school, wrote a number of poems sometimes read at modern Persian weddings. These include short blessings such as 'Wedding Bliss' and 'Words for a Wedding' and the lyrical ode 'Our Feast, Our Wedding'.

that he is to be a published novelist. In the ensuing celebration he wishes Baba could see him and he thinks of Rahim Khan's support when he started writing and of Hassan's praise for his storytelling skills. His book is published in the summer of 1989 and, at the same time, he and Soraya start trying to have a child.

A year passes and Soraya does not conceive. They have tests: no reason is found for their infertility so they commence treatment. This also fails to work and finally the doctor mentions adoption. However, Soraya does not want to adopt, she wants her own flesh and blood in her arms. Her father agrees, talking about bloodlines and ancestral lines: both his and Amir's. Amir wonders if the lack of fertility is a divine punishment for his past actions. Amir and Soraya buy a bigger house with the money from his books and get on with their lives, forgetting about children, but Amir feels their childlessness is an unspoken part of their marriage.

COMMENTARY

The courting and marriage ceremony of Amir and Soraya are very traditional, if shortened because of Baba's illness. This would seem to be Amir's final attempt to make his father proud of him and to show Baba that he can be a true Afghan.

The reoccurrence, during the ceremony, of the Afghan wedding song which was sung by the Russian guard during the escape from Afghanistan of Baba and Amir is a demonstration of the safety of the USA compared to Russian-occupied Afghanistan, but also a sign of continuity, of bringing the old country into the new. It shows Amir finally starting to grow into his heritage. The reappearance of this song also suggests that the past cannot be escaped. Thus when Amir and Soraya look at each other in the mirror, one of the most intimate moments of the ceremony, Amir is wondering about Hassan and 'whose face he [Hassan] had seen in the mirror under the veil? Whose henna-painted hands had he held?' (p. 149).

Baba's death follows quickly after the wedding. Baba is finally able to relinquish hold on life because he has seen his son become a man and knows that he will be taken care of. Baba's reading of Amir's stories at least partly lays to rest Amir's constant need to make his father proud of him. However, at the funeral, Amir realises how large a figure in his life his father has been and how large a gap is left to fill.

The general's migraines and Jamila's hypochondria are, like Baba's cancer, signs of the ill effect that living in the USA has on that generation of Afghans. However, along with the general being happy to use the welfare payments that are sent to him, we can see that Amir does not hold his new parents-in-law in the same esteem as he held Baba.

In contrast to her parents, both Amir and Soraya are happy and healthy. However, their mysterious infertility can be seen as another example of the Afghans not being able to thrive away from their own country. The revelation of their infertility is coupled with the news of Amir getting his first two novels published. As with the story of the tournament and Hassan's rape it would seem as though Amir has had to trade one success – his potential fatherhood – for another – the publishing deal. In addition, Amir's success is shown in contrast to a change in the fate of Afghanistan, from Russian occupation to civil war and infighting, suggesting that Amir's success is also at Afghanistan's expense.

> **CONTEXT**
>
> A migraine usually involves a combination of headache and nausea and, very often, a sensitivity to light. There are thought to be a number of different causes, although it has been found that genes can play a part in a person's likelihood of suffering from migraines. In adults it is a condition which afflicts far more women than men.

GLOSSARY

145 *ghazal* love song

145 **Ustad Sarahang** Afghan musician

147 *noor* light

149 *sholeh-goshti* flame-cooked meat

149 *attan* Afghan dance

153 *chila* wedding ring

154 **raga** Indian musical form

155 *maladies* illnesses

160 **Merlot** a red wine

160 *Mujahedin* a Muslim who is engaged in a holy war – used to refer to those who fought against the Soviets in Afghanistan

160 **Najibullah** the fourth and last president of the communist Democratic Republic of Afghanistan

160 **Tiananmen Square** large, open square in Beijing, China, site of prominent protests in 1989

161 *Kho dega!* So!

161 *alahoo* God

161 *nawasa* grandchild

Chapter 14

- It is June 2001 and Amir has just received a phone call from Rahim Khan.
- Amir and Soraya are still childless.
- Amir flies to Pakistan.

The story returns to June 2001 and the time of Rahim Khan's phone call to Amir mentioned in Chapter 1. As Amir puts down the phone Soraya asks him what is wrong and he informs her that he must go to Pakistan because Rahim Khan is sick. She asks if she should go with him, but he says he will go alone. He goes to Golden Gate Park to think and he watches kites flying. He thinks of Rahim Khan saying *'There is a way to be good again'* (p. 168) and realises that Khan has always known about the events in the alley.

Soraya arranges for her parents to stay with her while Amir is away. The past ten years have improved the relationship between her and her father. They take walks together and sometimes he sits in on her classes. That night in bed Amir again feels the issue of their childlessness as a weight on their marriage. Finally asleep he dreams of Hassan in the snow. A week later, Amir flies to Pakistan.

Commentary

This chapter marks the mid-point of the novel. It brings the story up to date with the events mentioned in Chapter 1 and finishes Amir's relation of his history. The story from here covers events after Rahim Khan's phone call in June 2001 from the perspective of Amir talking to us in December 2001: a period of six months.

The revelation that Rahim Khan has known about the secret Amir has been holding all these years is a powerful one. We already know from previous chapters that Hassan's rape weighs heavy on Amir and that he has tried, on a number of occasions, to find a way to atone. Finally, with this phone call from Rahim Khan, Amir is being offered a way to 'be good again' (p. 168).

Amir's and Soraya's childlessness remains a factor in their lives. This information is coupled with Amir dreaming of Hassan. The **juxtaposition** of these two passages suggests that Amir cannot have children of his own until his debt to Hassan has been paid and his guilt finally assuaged. The memories of Hassan's friendship and loyalty demonstrated by the repetition of the phrase 'For you, a thousand times over!' (p. 169) thus lends added poignancy to what Amir describes as the 'futility' (p. 169) of the act of lovemaking he has just performed with his wife.

CHAPTER 15

- Amir arrives in Pakistan and meets a very ill Rahim Khan.
- Rahim Khan recounts to Amir the terrible changes in Kabul.
- Rahim Khan is dying and he wishes Amir to perform a final favour for him.

Amir arrives in Peshawar and remembers it from his time there with his father. He is taken by taxi into a part of the town predominantly filled with Afghans. There he once again meets Rahim Khan whom he hasn't seen since 1981 when Amir and Baba left Kabul. The older man is incredibly thin and obviously ill.

At first they do not talk about Rahim Khan's illness. Amir talks about his marriage and they discuss Afghanistan and the rule of the Taliban. Rahim Khan provides him with examples of their brutality. He also explains how Kabul has changed since Amir left. He relates the initial rejoicing when the Taliban took over from the Alliance and how the Alliance had destroyed Baba's orphanage. Finally the conversation turns to Rahim Khan's health and the fact that he is dying and will not last the summer. Amir offers to take him back to the USA, but Rahim Khan turns him down. He had wanted to see Amir before he died, but he also has something to tell him.

Rahim Khan relates to Amir how he lived on in Baba's house after Amir and Baba left and for many of those years Hassan lived with

CONTEXT

Peshawar is a large city in Pakistan, close to the border with Afghanistan. At times in its history it was part of the Afghan empire and still has a large Afghan population. It was the first destination of most Afghans fleeing the Soviet invasion.

him. He explains that he is going to ask a favour of him, but first he is going to tell him all about Hassan.

COMMENTARY

This chapter opens with a rich description of Peshawar as a 'city bursting with sounds' (p. 171), '[r]ich scents, both pleasant and not so pleasant' (p. 171) and many different sights including 'carpet vendors, kabob stalls, [and] kids with dirt-caked hands selling cigarettes' (p. 171). This is reminiscent of Amir's earlier descriptions of the Kabul of his childhood but stands in stark contrast to the descriptions of that city in the chapters that follow.

The last time Amir and Rahim Khan spoke was over the death of Amir's father, Baba. Many times in the novel Amir comments on how he might have preferred to have Rahim Khan as his father, and now he finds this surrogate father is also dying. These deaths are the events which precipitate the changes in Amir from a scared boy into a strong man. To some extent, the death of Rahim Khan will be more significant, because he not only was a clearer guide for the young Amir, but also he possesses Amir's secret and so can provide the means to overcome it.

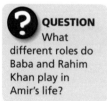

QUESTION
What different roles do Baba and Rahim Khan play in Amir's life?

The destruction of Baba's orphanage represents a **symbolic** second death of Amir's father and also can be as seen as a personal affront. The orphanage was a symbol for Amir of his father's strength and compassion. With its destruction, and the death of the children inside it, it is as though that aspect of Baba has also been destroyed. The death of children is also a personal tragedy for a man who remains childless. This is just one of the many instances in *The Kite Runner* where children are either threatened or actually hurt, their vulnerability forming a recurrent **motif** which does much to represent the breakdown of culture and family in Afghanistan over the period covered by the novel.

The end of this chapter sees the return of Hassan to the story as a character rather than just a symbol of Amir's guilt. Rahim Khan offers to present the story of Hassan and asks for a favour as a continuation of the promise of redemption which he made in his phone call. Amir's decision to listen to a story which he admits to himself he does not want to hear shows the opening up of his mind to the possibilities of change and redemption. He is finally taking advantage of a chance to make things right where he declined the chances he had at the time.

GLOSSARY

170 **Jamrud** a town on the edge of the Kyber Pass

170 **Cantonment** a semi-permanent military quarters or residential barracks

173 **INS** Immigration and Naturalization Service, a US government agency

173 **Ghazi** sports stadium in Kabul named after Sardar Shah Mahmud Khan Ghazi, prime minister of Afghanistan from May 1946 to 7 September 1953

174 **Deh-Mazang** town near Kabul

175 **caracul** a type of coarse wool

176 **melancholic** tending to be sad or depressed

CHAPTER 16

- Rahim Khan relates the story of what has happened to him since Amir last saw him.
- Rahim Khan brought Hassan and his wife to live with him.
- Hassan's mother, Sanaubar, returned.
- Hassan and his wife had a son, Sohrab.

Rahim Khan relates the story of how in 1986 he went to Hazarajat to find Hassan. Most of his friends and family had been killed or had fled the country and he was feeling lonely. Additionally, his arthritis had made it difficult to maintain the house. With the news of Baba's death he finally decided to find Ali and Hassan.

A short search led him to Hassan who was living in a small village outside Bamiyan. Hassan introduced him to his visibly pregnant wife, Farzana, then told him that Ali had been killed by a landmine two years before. After more conversation and dinner, Rahim Khan asked Hassan and his wife to return to the house with him. Hassan refused because of his ties to his village and the nearby town.

CONTEXT

Bamiyan is the largest town in Hazarajat. It was made famous by the ancient giant statues known as the Buddhas of Bamiyan which were carved into a mountainside there. These were destroyed by the Taliban in 2001.

Following dinner Hassan asked Rahim Khan all about Amir and his new life in the USA. He asked about Baba: when Rahim Khan told him of his death, Hassan cried. In the morning, Hassan told Rahim Khan that he and his wife had changed their minds and would come back to Kabul with him.

On returning to Baba's house Hassan would not move into any of the many empty rooms but insisted on living in the hut where he had been born. After that Hassan and his wife took over all the cooking and cleaning duties. In the late autumn, Farzana gave birth to a stillborn girl whom Hassan buried in the yard. Despite the war, the three of them made a haven out of the house and its walled garden. In early 1990, Farzana became pregnant again and a strange woman appeared at the house. She was weak from starvation and her face had been cut. She was Sanaubar, Hassan's mother. On hearing this news Hassan ran from the house. However, he returned next morning and accepted his mother back into his family.

Hassan and his wife nursed his mother back to health and she in turn delivered Hassan's son, Sohrab. Sanaubar later died when Sohrab was four, simply failing to wake from sleep. She was buried in the old cemetery by the pomegranate tree. In the two years that followed, Hassan tried to give his son a normal life – going to the zoo and cinema, playing with slingshot and kite, and reading stories from books.

Then, in 1996, when Rahim Khan returned home from celebrating the defeat of the Mujahedin by the Taliban, he found Hassan looking serious and worried about the fate of the Hazara now that the Taliban were taking over. A few weeks later, Rahim Khan relates, kite fighting was banned by the Taliban, and two years later, in 1998, they massacred the Hazaras in Mazar-i-Sharif, a Shi'a city in northern Afghanistan.

CHECK THE BOOK

In *Swallows of Kabul* (2004), Yasmina Khadra explores in greater depth the events in Afghanistan which Rahim Khan relates in this chapter.

COMMENTARY

This chapter is the story which Rahim Khan relates to Amir represented as a **first-person narrative**. It is the only chapter in the novel not told from Amir's perspective and the first time we hear a different voice. This voice is different in tone and in sentence construction from Amir's voice, pointing up the particular style of

Amir's passages. Phrases such as 'Allah forgive me' (p. 178) and the use of the word 'would' in sentences such as 'I would take a walk', 'I would pray *namaz*' or 'I would rise in the morning' (p. 178) suggest a more considered and thoughtful voice than Amir's.

Just as Rahim Khan is Amir's surrogate father and the man who holds the key to his redemption, so Baba was a second father to Hassan. Hassan's return to Kabul on the news of Baba's death reflects Amir's return to Pakistan because of Rahim Khan's illness. Both men see a chance to redeem themselves at the point at which they lose the support of their father figures.

In Rahim Khan's story we discover that Hassan has married and we also see the return of his mother, Sanaubar. Women have been largely absent from the novel, and feature mostly at moments of transition. The mothers of both Hassan and Amir leave the **narrative** at the moment they give birth. Soraya enters the story as Baba dies and Sanaubar only re-enters the story after Hassan has returned to Kabul following the deaths of Ali and Baba. Still, this is a male-centred narrative as we see when Hassan's daughter is stillborn but his son, Sohrab, survives.

Hassan's son's name is taken from the storybook which Amir used to read to Hassan. This is another example of the importance of stories in the novel but also a harking back to a happier past and another example of Hassan's enduring loyalty to Amir. Rahim Khan describes the young boy as an avid reader, like Amir, but also a talented kite runner and slingshot shooter like Hassan. With these two attributes it seems as though Sohrab is being described as the son of both Hassan and Amir; the son Amir has failed to have and the fulfilment of the potential which Amir's actions denied Hassan.

Hassan's rebuilding of the 'Wall of Ailing Corn' (p. 183) is **symbolic** of trying to rebuild what he used to have, as well as building a boundary between the haven that is Baba's house and the war in the outside world. The banning of kite fighting is a symbolic destruction of the happier remains of Amir's past – and the massacre of the Hazaras in Mazar-i-Sharif. This final event demonstrates how the prejudice against the Hazaras which was evident during Amir's childhood – especially in the attitudes of Assef and his friends, but

> **CONTEXT**
>
> Ali is reported as having been killed by a landmine. This war a favoured weapon of the Mujahedin during their conflict with the Soviets, often planted on their behalf by children. Reports estimate that over 10 million landmines remained in the ground after the Soviet retreat, that 25,000 Afghans have been killed by them and that, of the remainder, nearly 4 per cent of all Afghans have been injured by landmines.

also in those of ordinary people – has become engrained at a higher level and has now led to violence and murder.

GLOSSARY

178 *chai* spiced tea

180 *Arg* a large Persian citadel

183 *burqa* a traditional item of Muslim clothing for women of this area, which covers the head, face and body

185 *isfand* plant burned to create smoke to ward off bad luck

185 *Sasa* grandmother

CHAPTER 17

- Rahim Khan gives Amir a letter from Hassan.
- Hassan and his wife have been murdered by the Taliban and their son, Sohrab, is now in an orphanage.
- Rahim Khan asks Amir to retrieve Sohrab and informs him that Hassan was his half-brother.

Following Rahim Khan's story, Amir asks if Hassan is still living in the house. The older man hands him an envelope. It contains a Polaroid photograph of a man Amir recognises as Hassan and a small boy who must be Sohrab. There is also a letter from Hassan. In the letter Hassan talks about his life in Taliban-controlled Kabul, about his son, and he sends his wishes to see Amir again. He describes himself as Amir's 'old faithful friend' (p. 191).

After Amir has read the letter, Rahim Khan informs him that it was written six months previously when he left to go to Pakistan. A month after that a neighbour in Kabul rang to inform him that Hassan and Farzana had both been killed by the Taliban who believed that they were living in the house illegally. The Taliban now occupy the house and Sohrab has been sent to live in an orphanage.

Having told him all this, Rahim Khan asks Amir for a favour. He wants Amir to go to Kabul and bring Sohrab back to Pakistan. He tells Amir that there is an American family in Peshawar who will adopt the boy. Amir does not want to go and offers to pay for someone to go and fetch Sohrab. Rahim Khan quotes a conversation with Amir's father in which Baba felt that 'a boy who won't stand up for himself becomes a man who can't stand up to anything' (p. 194). Rahim Khan expresses his worry that this is what has happened to Amir. He then continues by explaining to Amir that Ali was infertile and that Baba was really Hassan's father, Amir's brother. Hassan never knew. Amir is angered by this news and by the fact that it has been kept from him for so long. Rahim Khan reminds him of the shame of the situation but Amir will not listen and storms from the apartment.

COMMENTARY

Following his story, Rahim Khan gives Amir a photograph of Hassan and Sohrab and a letter from him. The presence of the photograph allows the story of Hassan to be brought up to date, with a physical representation of him in adulthood. The letter, as with Rahim Khan's story, gives us a separate voice from Amir's with a different mode of speech. For example the opening 'In the name of Allah the most beneficent, the most merciful, Amir agha, with my deepest respects' (p. 189) is a much more formal and convoluted way of writing than we see from Amir. However, this mode of communication finally allows Hassan to reveal his love for and loyalty to Amir in his own voice, rather than merely just in Amir's interpretation.

In Hassan's letter he touches on many of the same things we have heard in Amir's story. This verifies that these things – the cemetery, the pomegranate tree, the storybook – were as significant to Hassan as Amir has claimed. He also brings our story of Kabul up to date and highlights the differences between what they experienced in their childhood and how life is now. Hassan stayed behind and has grown and changed with his country. Amir, in contrast, having left in 1981 is in a state of suspended animation with his development as an Afghan stunted at an early age.

The death of Hassan affects him at least as profoundly as the death of his father and the news of Rahim Khan's imminent illness. As with other moments of stress in the novel, the structure of the

> **CONTEXT**
>
> Following the decades of war in Afghanistan, and the brutal regime of the Taliban, there are a large number of children without parents. These orphans have become the focus of many aid organisations from all over the world, but providing food and shelter for them all is a huge problem.

language breaks down and Amir can interject nothing more than denials, attempting to hold back his emotions about the loss he is feeling – both in terms of Hassan's death but also in terms of his chance for atonement. It means that he can now never seek forgiveness from Hassan for what he did as a child. However, as with the death and illness of the other two main influences in his life, this is another spur forcing Amir towards maturity and towards accepting his inheritance.

Rahim Khan's request that Amir go to Kabul and rescue Sohrab is Amir's chance to finally make penance for what he didn't do for Hassan. The fact that the boy is in an orphanage is a reference back to Baba's orphanage. Saving Sohrab is therefore revealed as something Baba would have done and something which Amir can do to finally become the man his father wished him to be, as well as repay his debt to Hassan.

In the final part of this chapter, the web of responsibilities between Baba, Amir, Hassan and Sohrab is made all the clearer when Rahim Khan reveals that Hassan was Baba's illegitimate son, and therefore Amir's half-brother. This information about Hassan's parentage harks back to the conversations about bloodlines in Chapter 13 and the importance to Afghans of knowing who their parents and ancestors are. It is this attachment which Rahim Khan hopes will convince Amir to do as he is asked.

CHECK THE POEM

Illegitimacy has always been a theme of literature, even as far back as Robert Burns's poem, 'Address to an Illegitimate Child' (1785).

GLOSSARY

188 **Urdu** official language of Pakistan

192 **herringbone vest** a waistcoat decorated with a black-and-white zigzag pattern

---

CHAPTER 18

- Amir considers the news that Hassan was his half-brother.
- He wonders if his betrayal of Hassan led to his friend's death.
- Amir makes the decision to go to Kabul to find his nephew.

Amir walks to a samovar house (a tea shop) and orders a cup of tea. He sits and considers the new information that Hassan was his half-brother. He remembers the affection that Baba had for the other boy, the birthday gifts and Baba's anger when Amir asked about getting new servants. Amir considers the possibility that if he had not betrayed Hassan, Ali and his son may now be still alive in the USA. He realises that with this new information he cannot refuse Rahim Khan's request. He must go to Kabul and find the boy who is his nephew.

COMMENTARY

As Amir walks the streets trying to understand the fact that Hassan was actually his brother he realises that he is not so different from his father: 'As it turned out, Baba and I were more alike that I'd ever known' (p. 197). They both had a secret with regard to their Hazara servants. In Amir's case it was the betrayal of Hassan by not helping him during his rape; for Baba it was the knowledge that he had slept with Ali's wife and was Hassan's father.

However, Amir realises that he denied his responsibility to Hassan while Baba did his best to make amends by taking care of both Ali and his son and trying to treat Hassan as kindly as he treated Amir. Amir now understands the reasons behind Baba's fondness for Hassan, the way he would treat both boys equally, the offence he took when Amir wanted to get new servants and the sorrow he felt when Ali and Hassan left.

CONTEXT

Lollywood (p. 196), the term coined for the Pakistan film industry, based in Lahore (hence the leading 'L'), produces films in a number of languages, including Pashto, making the Pashtun-dominated Afghanistan a key export market. However, the industry is in decline, finding it impossible to compete with America's Hollywood or India's Bollywood.

CHAPTER 19

- Amir returns to Taliban-held Afghanistan to rescue Sohrab.
- Farid, the driver, accuses Amir of always having been a visitor in his own country.
- Wahid, Farid's brother, gives Amir all the food he and his family have to eat.
- Farid agrees to help Amir once he realises the reason for his return.

In the car on the way back into Afghanistan, Amir once more suffers from car sickness. The man who is driving, Farid, offers him a lemon as a cure, disdaining the need for any fancy American medicine. Farid had been introduced to Amir by Rahim Kahn. The older man had also helped Amir to change his money and to purchase a convincing, Taliban-friendly, artificial beard.

? QUESTION
The concept of *watan* (homeland) is crucial in *The Kite Runner*. In what varying ways is it presented in the novel?

On entering Afghanistan, Amir feels out of place in his own country with the ruins and scars of twenty years of war having changed it so much. He relates this to Farid who is scornful of him for what he imagines was Amir's easy childhood, his servants and rich family, and his life in the USA. He taunts Amir, saying that he has always been a tourist in Afghanistan, with the real people having always lived much harder lives. He asks if Amir has come back to sell off his father's land, take the money and run back to America. Amir cannot reply because he has to ask Farid to stop the car so he can be sick.

Farid takes Amir into Jalalabad to his brother's house. After welcoming him and making him comfortable, Wahid, Farid's brother, asks why Amir has come back to Afghanistan. Farid again dismisses Amir's reasons, suggesting he has returned for monetary gain only. Wahid turns on his brother in anger and apologises to Amir for his brother's lack of respect. Amir explains his desire to find Sohrab and take him back to Peshawar. Wahid expresses his pride in Amir's journey and Farid cannot meet Amir's gaze. Maryam, Wahid's wife, then provides Amir with food. He tries to offer the food to the family but Wahid says that they have already eaten. As he eats he sees Wahid's children looking at his digital watch so after dinner, with their father's permission, he gives them the watch. However, they soon lose interest in it.

Later, as they are going to sleep, Farid protests that Amir should have told him the real reason why he has come back and offers to help him find Sohrab. Amir sleeps and dreams of Hassan being shot, kneeling in the street outside his old house; he wakes with an urge to scream. He goes outside and contemplates his feelings on being back in Afghanistan. As he is about to return inside he hears Maryam and Wahid arguing about the fact that Wahid has given their guest all the food in the house. Amir realises that it was the

food the children were looking at, not his watch. The next morning
Amir thanks Wahid as they leave. He is saddened by the fact that
the children are too hungry to chase after the car but reflects that
earlier in the morning he had once again hidden a handful of money
under a mattress.

COMMENTARY

The stories of Rahim Khan and Hassan may have informed Amir
about the state of Afghanistan, but he is still shocked and saddened.
This is the country he abandoned, and his feelings for the country have
been bound up with his feelings over his relationships with both Baba
and Hassan. Seeing the country in this state is like seeing his internal
landscape ravaged by all the years of guilt. This is an association Amir
makes clear when he comments, 'My mother had died on this soil. And
on this soil, I had fought for my father's love' (p. 210).

Once again Amir is car sick while being driven to Jalalabad. This
sickness seems to be caused, at least in part, by the country itself
because we are only told about him being sick when travelling
through Afghanistan. It is a continued sign of his weakness: the
reaction that he has to his own country ties in with Farid's
comments about him being a tourist in his own land. This issue is
discussed further in **Extended commentary 3.**

The welcome Amir receives from Wahid and his family is in
contrast to Farid's initial suspicion of Amir's motives for returning.
Wahid's reaction is representative of traditional Afghan hospitality
proving that it still remains in the country despite the decades of
war. Farid is a product of the new Afghanistan and is reminiscent of
the cynical Karim, the truck driver who helped Baba and Amir
escape from the country in the first place.

However, for all that Wahid's welcome is warm and traditionally
generous, the fact that making Amir welcome leaves no food for the
rest of the family shows how difficult it is for Wahid to maintain his
traditional values during such impoverished times. Upon realising
that he has eaten all Wahid's food, Amir feels guilty, but it is a sign
that he has not yet achieved the stature of his father that he does not
approach Wahid with his gift of money but instead hides it under a

CHECK THE BOOK
The concept of
'returning' is one
which runs through
the whole novel.
Amir spends much
of his adult life
revisiting the events
of the past –
including the whole
narration of his story
– but it is only in his
physical return to
Afghanistan that he
can finally make
restitution. *The
Odyssey*, by Homer,
is perhaps the most
famous story about
returning home and
the perils and
possibilities of the
journey.

QUESTION
Hosseini uses many **images** and **motifs** from earlier in the novel as he relates Amir's stay with Wahid and his family. What are they and how do they affect the progression of the **narrative**?

mattress. As Amir comments, this is the same method he used to disgrace Hassan so many years ago. As a **symbol**, leaving the money for a good purpose shows the penance which Amir is trying to perform; however, it could also be suggested that it shows a continued level of cowardice and a refusal to face up to matters.

GLOSSARY

201 **Hindu Kush** mountain range separating Pakistan and Afghanistan

201 **Tajik** someone from Tajikistan

202 *jihad* holy war

202 *Shari'a* Muslim legal system

202 **ruminate** to think over

202 **rationalize** to provide reasons for a course of action

203 *mehmanis* parties

205 **dilapidated** falling apart from age and misuse

205 **adobe** building material made from sand, clay, water, straw and sometimes dung

206 *hijab* head scarf, sometimes with attached veil

CHAPTER 20

- Kabul has been severely damaged by twenty years of war.
- The Taliban patrol the streets looking for people to punish.
- Amir discovers that Sohrab has been sold by the orphanage director to a prominent member of the Taliban.

Despite Farid's warning, Amir is shocked by the devastation he sees on the journey from Jalalabad to Kabul. The road is potholed by bombs and mines, and villages are burned and empty. Farid, however, is more friendly now that he knows Amir's reasons for coming home.

On arriving in Kabul, Amir is saddened because it has been reduced to 'rubble and beggars' (p. 214). Everything Amir remembers has been damaged or demolished. All the trees have been cut down either for firewood or to prevent snipers from having somewhere to hide. Farid stops the car so Amir can walk in a street he remembers. It no longer smells of cooking lamb but of the diesel from generators. As they stand there a group of Taliban drive past in a pickup truck. Amir watches as they drive past and Farid warns him never to stare at them because that is all the provocation they need to attack someone.

A nearby beggar confirms this advice. Amir gives the beggar some money and asks about the orphanage that Sohrab was taken to. In their conversation the beggar reveals that he used to teach at the University and that he knew Amir's mother. He tells Amir what he remembers of her and Amir treasures the information. Leaving the beggar behind, Farid and Amir follow his directions to the orphanage. Amir shows the Polaroid photo of Sohrab to the man who answers the door, but the man protests that the child is not there. Finally, Amir informs the man who he is and why he's there and the man lets him in, revealing that he does know the child Amir is talking about.

The man introduces himself as Zaman, the director of the orphanage. He shows them around the building, which was originally a storage warehouse. He explains that there is a shortage of food, water and blankets. Finally, he apologises to Amir saying that he may be too late to help Sohrab. He takes Amir and Farid to his office and informs Amir that Sohrab was taken away by a Taliban official a month earlier; the man comes regularly with money and buys a boy or a girl. Farid is so angered by this selling of the orphans that he leaps over the desk and tries to strangle Zaman, but Amir stops him by warning that the orphans are watching him. Zaman explains that he does what he does because it is the only way to get money to feed the remaining children. Amir asks who the man is who bought Sohrab, and Zaman replies that he will find him at the next day's football match wearing black sunglasses. Amir and Farid leave.

COMMENTARY

Continuing Amir's education about the real state of his home country, Kabul is even more damaged than Amir could have

CHECK THE BOOK

In *The Bookseller of Kabul* (2003), Asne Seierstad provides a vivid picture of life in Kabul under the Taliban and in the years since.

CHECK THE FILM

Slumdog Millionaire (2008) features a comparable situation where children of the Mumbai slums in India are 'rescued' and employed as beggars by a corrupt orphanage owner. Some of the children are cruelly disfigured in order to attract more sympathy and be more profitable.

imagined. The city which is the backdrop to all his childhood memories is almost unrecognisable. By revisiting this city and re-educating himself – seeing it, as he says, 'through Farid's eyes' (p. 213) – he is bringing himself closer to what remains of his Afghan heritage. He uses rich **imagery** to describe this new version of Kabul in order to evoke the pain and sadness he feels in what he sees. He describes children playing amongst 'jagged stumps of brick and stone' (p. 215), recalling the time when he used to play in the city himself, and talks about the city as an old friend who is now 'homeless and destitute' (p. 216). This contrasts with his descriptions of the city he remembers from his childhood and, in doing so, suggests the trauma of seeing the city in such a state.

Upon arriving in the city he sees the Taliban in the flesh for the first time. While everyone else looks away, Amir stares at them. This reinforces Farid's earlier comment about Amir being a tourist in his own country. He watches the Taliban as if they were an item on the news. He still cannot entirely connect with the reality of the situation in his country.

The appearance of the beggar seems a remarkable coincidence but is, as with Wahid's generosity, a sign of the old Afghanistan still existing despite the terrible conditions and the wars of the previous three decades. It is also a **symbol** of how little regard the Taliban have for education and the tragedy of modern Afghanistan where educated men are reduced to begging.

With Baba's orphanage having been destroyed, Sohrab has been kept in a converted warehouse in one of the most badly damaged parts of the city. It is an unsuitable building and the children are kept in rooms with 'no floor covering but matted carpets and windows shuttered with sheets of plastic' (p. 222). As with the news of the original orphanage having been destroyed, this is a personal affront to a man who so dearly wants children and cannot have them. Increasingly the state of Afghanistan seems to be becoming part of Amir's divine punishment both for his offences against Hassan but also for deserting Afghanistan. With no people like Baba and his offspring to provide and protect the country and its inhabitants, Afghanistan has been left as vulnerable and fatherless as its orphans. The director's tales of the Taliban's crimes and his own compromised morality are simply extensions of this idea.

CONTEXT

Kabul University was established in 1931, but was almost completely closed during the rule of the Taliban. It has since started to function once more as a university, and is slowly rebuilding and restaffing.

GLOSSARY

214 **tabla** a type of drum

222 **yateem** orphans

CHAPTER 21

- Amir's old neighbourhood is largely undamaged because it has been taken over by the new leaders.
- Amir climbs the hill to the old cemetery and discovers that the pomegranate tree has died.
- Amir and Farid watch the man in sunglasses – the man who bought Sohrab from the orphanage – stone two people to death at a football match.

Farid and Amir head back through the devastated city to the Wazir Akbar Khan district where Amir grew up. He is surprised to see it is largely untouched but Farid explains this is because it is where the powerful people live now: the Taliban as well as the Arabs, Chechens and Pakistanis who are the real power behind the Taliban. Amir then spots his street and they turn into it.

A memory intrudes as Amir recalls how he and Hassan played in the grounds of Baba's house, pretending to be great explorers. Back in the here and now, Amir walks up to look through the gate of his old house. It is run down and unkempt. A jeep is parked in the driveway instead of the black Mustang he expects to see. Farid calls him back, but Amir cannot tear himself away. He feels that he wants to go in and resume his childhood life. Finally, he returns to the car but asks Farid to wait because he has something more to see. Farid advises it is better to forget but Amir says he does not want to forget any more. Amir gets badly out of breath climbing the hill to the old cemetery. The pomegranate tree has died and will never bear fruit again, but he finds the inscription of his and Hassan's names still on the trunk. He sits under the tree and looks out over the city and remembers how it used to be. Eventually a honk of the horn calls him back down to the car.

CONTEXT

Although the Taliban ruled Afghanistan for many years, they were never acknowledged by the United Nations as the legitimate power in the country. This remained the Northern Alliance, also known as the United Islamic Front for the Salvation of Afghanistan. This was an organisation of disparate groups who banded together to fight the Taliban. They formed the basis of the current democratic government.

Farid and Amir check in to a hotel with very poor facilities and Farid fetches them food which is as tasty as it ever was. As they prepare for sleep Farid tells a common kind of Afghan joke about Mullah Nasruddin. Amir laughs at the joke but also at how Afghan humour has managed to remain largely unchanged. Just before sleep Farid finally asks Amir why he is doing so much for this one boy. Particularly, Farid asks, for a Shi'a. Amir does not reply.

The next day they go to the football stadium and watch the match played on the dusty, pitted field. At half time two pickup trucks come out: a man and a woman in the back of them are lowered into pits behind one set of goalposts. A cleric recites a prayer from the Koran and Amir remembers Baba's fear of what would happen to Afghanistan if the religious elements ever took over. The cleric then denounces the pair in the holes as adulterers and declares that they must be stoned for their crime. At this a tall man dressed all in white and wearing black sunglasses emerges from one truck and proceeds to stone the two to death. The bodies are put back in the trucks and the holes partly filled. The second half of the football match then commences. Farid makes arrangements for Amir to meet the man in the sunglasses and an appointment is made for three o'clock that afternoon.

COMMENTARY

Amir finds that his old neighbourhood is largely unchanged because the Taliban have chosen this as their area in which to settle. This reinforces Farid's earlier comments about Amir's privileged upbringing. If the place where he grew up is considered the preferred place by those who could choose any part of the city, then it shows how impressive a part of the town it is. Amir stares at his house for a long time, longer than Farid is comfortable with. This is part of the process Amir is going through, reconnecting with the childhood he has been running away from all his life. He now realises that he no longer wants to forget the past but to embrace it and move forward. This is a demonstrable step in his healing process.

Amir arrives at the pomegranate tree out of breath, 'each ragged breath … like inhaling fire' (p. 230), showing how he is an older person than the one who used to come up here. When he arrives it is to find that the tree is now dead. The tree was a **symbol** of the close relationship between Amir and Hassan. Its death now symbolises the end of that physical relationship with Hassan's death. However, the inscription

CONTEXT

Unlike other sports and activities, football was not banned under the Taliban regime. Players were banned from wearing shorts, however, and when a team came from Pakistan they were arrested for wearing shorts and had their heads shaved as punishment before being sent home.

CHECK THE BOOK

Michael Frayn's novel *Spies* (2002), although focusing on the Second World War, also has the character looking back on events of his childhood in the context of wartime. It too contains passages from the present, with the **narrator** as an older man.

that Amir carved, with his and Hassan's names, is still there, showing that their friendship can exist beyond the barrier of death.

The spectacle of the stoning taking place in the middle of the football match finally brings home to Amir the situation he is in and the state of his homeland. The fact that the man he needs to meet is the one doing the stoning makes it all the more real. The **juxtaposition** of these two events suggests that the stoning would be seen in the same light as the football – as a sport – and the crowd's reactions uphold this idea as they watch and shout comments. The suggestion is that the Afghan people have become used to the violence and now view it as an ordinary occurrence. Amir reports that the 'crowd made a startled "OH!" sound' (p. 237) during the stoning, but nothing more. Only Amir has any strong reaction, hiding his face and waiting for it to be over. It is a naive and childlike response, connecting back to the Amir whose development as an Afghan stopped when he was still a child and unlike those who stayed behind, has not been desensitised to the constant violence. This continues the theme of the return journey being Amir's chance to finally grow up and reminds us that he is still struggling to do so.

The Talib who does the stoning is dressed all in white and wearing John Lennon-style sunglasses. This is **ironic** as white is a symbol of peace and purity – attributes which are at odds with the man's actions. In addition, the sunglasses are symbolic of a decadent Western consumer society, but are being worn by a member of a religion which bans all such things. As such the Talib is shown as a hypocritical figure as well as a cruel one.

> **CONTEXT**
>
> Death by stoning was the usual punishment for adultery under the Taliban. Despite the ending of their regime and the passing of equality laws, the practice of stoning women to death, for a variety of reasons, has sadly continued.

GLOSSARY

228 **semilunar** half-moon shaped

229 **Rorschach inkblot** random shapes used by psychologists to provoke unconscious reactions to help diagnose patients

231 *azan* Islamic call to prayer

231 *mueszzin* the person at the mosque who performs the call to prayer

232 **Panjsher Valley** a region of Afghanistan in the north

237 **John Lennon sunglasses** small round sunglasses such as those worn by John Lennon of the pop group The Beatles

CHAPTER 22

- Amir meets the man in sunglasses who has bought Sohrab.
- The man reveals himself to be Assef, the bully from Amir's childhood.
- Assef fights with Amir and hurts him badly, but Amir is saved by Sohrab and his slingshot.

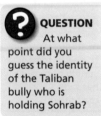

QUESTION
At what point did you guess the identity of the Taliban bully who is holding Sohrab?

The meeting between Amir and the man in the sunglasses takes place in a big house in Amir's old neighbourhood. Farid waits in the car while Amir bangs on the gates and is admitted by two men carrying Kalashnikov rifles. He goes in, unsure if he will come out again. He sits inside the house and waits and worries. Finally, the man in white comes in, still wearing his sunglasses, and sits down opposite Amir, watching him and not speaking. The man's clothes still have blood on them from the stoning. The man greets Amir and then gets one of the guards to remove Amir's false beard. The man asks if Amir enjoyed the show at the stadium. When Amir shows little enthusiasm the man starts to talk about the massacre at Mazir and how much he enjoyed killing the Hazaras there.

Amir gathers the courage to mention Sohrab. The man does not respond but instead directs insults at the USA. He informs Amir that he could have him shot for treason for abandoning Afghanistan all those years ago. He asks if Amir is frightened and Amir admits that he is. Amir loses himself in thoughts of Soraya until the man asks if he wants to see Sohrab. Amir says that he does: a guard comes back in leading a small boy made up with mascara and rouge and with bells on his ankles. Still, the resemblance to a young Hassan is remarkable and disorientates Amir. One of the guards presses a button and as music plays they force the boy to dance for them.

When the dance has finished the man in the sunglasses picks up the boy and holds him on his lap. He then asks Amir what happened to his father. Amir realises that he has been recognised. The man takes off the glasses and Amir realises that this cruel man is his childhood bully, Assef. He asks why Amir has really come back; Amir repeats that he has come for the boy and offers to pay for him, but Assef refuses. Assef tells how he came to be in the position he now holds.

Assef continues to ask why Amir wants the boy, but Amir refuses to tell him. Finally Assef gives the boy to Amir to take away. However, as Amir reaches the door, Assef announces there will be a price. The price is to finish their childhood fight. Assef instructs the guards to leave the room, saying that only one man will emerge and even if it is Amir he is to be allowed to pass. He tells them to leave Sohrab so that he can watch.

QUESTION
The Kite Runner is largely a novel about sons and fathers. In what ways is Sohrab like Hassan?

It is Amir's first fight and he remembers it only in patches. Assef uses his brass knuckles, just as he used to, to beat Amir. Yet as Amir gets beaten he starts to laugh. This angers Assef more and more. However, just before he administers a final killing blow, Sohrab asks him to stop. Assef looks up to see the boy holding up his slingshot with a brass ball in the cup. When Assef lunges for Sohrab, the boy fires the ball and hits Assef in the left eye. Sohrab then steps over the incapacitated Assef and helps Amir to his feet. The two escape past the surprised guards. Sohrab helps Amir to the front door where Farid comes up to carry him to the truck. He quickly loads the severely wounded Amir into the truck and together the three of them make their escape.

COMMENTARY

This chapter sees Amir badly frightened at the situation he finds himself in but finally standing up and emulating both his father's and Hassan's acts of bravery. His journey of self-discovery has finally brought him to a confrontation with his own childhood fears in the form of the bully, Assef, who is now a leading Talib.

It seems appropriate that Assef has risen to this position of authority. In a country where social norms have broken down, it is likely that those in power behave as sociopaths. Assef is clearly in his element and fulfilling a role for which he was always suited. He has finally found a way to emulate the man he earlier declared as a hero, Adolf Hitler.

When Sohrab enters the room Amir once more comments on how much the boy looks like his father. This acts as a reminder to Amir of the attack which Assef perpetrated against Hassan, and so spurs him on. By fighting Assef in order to save Sohrab he can also finally fight to save Hassan and repay his debt to his former servant. In describing the boy, Amir repeats some of the descriptive language he used to first describe Hassan. He mentions the 'Chinese doll face of my childhood' (p. 244), but the contextual language is harder and less poetic, reflecting the harsh circumstances in which he is encountering Sohrab.

Upon first meeting Assef he notices that there is blood on his white clothes from the stoning. This alters the **symbolism** of these clothes from purity and peace, to being like a butcher's apron. There is also the **image** of blood on white sheets associated with the loss of virginity, suggesting that by engaging in the fight with Assef, Amir is losing the last of his innocence and naivety.

By going through with the fight, Amir is finally able to lay his demons to rest and, just as Assef started to laugh when a beating helped him pass an excruciatingly painful kidney stone, so Amir starts to laugh as the beating he receives from Assef finally banishes the pain and guilt he has felt ever since Hassan's rape. It is the beating he has felt he deserved ever since that day and which he tried to provoke from Hassan by throwing pomegranates at him. Amir is once more rescued by a boy with a slingshot in a scene which harks back to the first aborted fight between Amir and Assef. However, in this case, Amir has taken full part in the fight and has no reason to be ashamed. Sohrab then actually fires the slingshot and performs the action that his father threatened Assef with all those years ago. This ends a battle which started in Chapter 5, showing the circular nature of the **narrative**.

> **? QUESTION**
> Recurring events, returning and cycles are all important in this novel. In what ways does the plot of *The Kite Runner* repeat various events?

GLOSSARY

244 *rupia* Indian currency
244 *pirhan-tumban* traditional Afghan dress
245 *dil-roba* an Indian stringed instrument
248 **kidney stones** small stones of calcium which can form in the kidney and cause acute pain while being passed from the body
253 *Bas* enough
254 **vitreous fluid** thick liquid inside the eyeball
254 *Bia* come (with me)

CHAPTER 23

- Amir is in hospital after his beating.
- Rahim Khan has left to die in peace and there is no sign of the adoptive parents he promised for Sohrab.
- Amir decides to take Sohrab with him to Islamabad while he considers what to do with him.

Amir floats in and out of unconsciousness with people asking him about his pain and his mental awareness. He does not remember what has happened or why he finds it painful to talk. He is being treated by a woman called Aisha but he has trouble knowing where he is or what is happening. He dreams of Baba wrestling the bear and Baba turns into Amir. He wakes to see Farid by his bedside. Amir recognises Farid and remembers the sound of bells before he passes out again.

When Amir recovers enough awareness he discovers he has needed surgery and his jaws are wired together. He is in a hospital in Peshawar. He has suffered several very severe injuries. One of these caused his upper lip to split down the middle leaving him with a scar.

The next day Farid and Sohrab come to visit. Amir introduces himself to the boy who has heard about him from his father. Amir asks about Rahim Khan, but he has disappeared leaving a letter and a key for Amir. The letter confirms that Rahim Khan knew Amir's secret but asks him not to be so hard on himself. It explains that his father was torn in his love for the two boys, and because he could not love Hassan openly he took it out on Amir. He talks more about Baba and then informs Amir that he has left some money for him to cover his expenses. He has left Peshawar to face his death alone and asks Amir not to look for him. Amir ponders the letter and when Aisha offers him a morphine injection, he agrees.

As Amir recovers Farid suggests that they leave Peshawar as soon as possible because the Taliban will be looking for him. Amir agrees but asks Farid to find the adoptive parents for Sohrab that Rahim Khan mentioned to him.

CONTEXT

When Amir wakes in the hospital he is bombarded with medical terms: hemorrhage splenectomy, pneumothorax. As with the terms surrounding Baba's cancer these are a sign that Amir has once again left behind the barbarism of Afghanistan for the more civilised world beyond its borders.

Sohrab and Amir play cards and talk about Hassan. Amir admits he was not as good a friend to Hassan as he could have been but asks to be Sohrab's friend. That night Amir walks for the first time since his beating and the next day he plans to leave the hospital and head home. However, Farid arrives to inform him that the adoptive parents do not exist. Amir determines to take the boy with him to Islamabad while he decides what to do.

COMMENTARY

When Amir dreams of himself wrestling the bear we can see how he has finally achieved, in his own mind at least, the stature of his father. By standing up to Assef, Amir has found a way to be the man his father always wanted him to be. Amir's split lip shows that, from his battle, he has come to resemble Hassan, his half-brother, making them almost like twins. This is a very physical sign that Amir has been able to repay his debts to Hassan.

Rahim Khan's letter is his final communication and the sign of his ultimate death. With Amir having achieved his growth into a man it is fitting that the last part of his childhood is sloughed off. In the letter Khan confirms what Amir has already been thinking about with regard to his father's guilt over the fathering of Hassan.

When Farid uses the phrase 'For you a thousand times over' (p. 266), echoing Hassan, it demonstrates the loyalty that Farid now feels for Amir. However, unlike with Hassan, this is a loyalty which Amir has earned through his actions, much in the same way as Baba would garner the respect of people around him. On the journey from Peshawar to Islamabad which occurs at the end of this chapter, Amir is not reported to suffer from car sickness. It seems that, in facing his childhood fears and overcoming them, he has cured this weakness as well.

GLOSSARY

256 **Clark Gable** American actor from the first half of the twentieth century, famous for his well-trimmed, thin moustache

259 **abdominal** to do with the stomach

259 **hemorrhage** bleed

259 **splenectomy** operation to remove the spleen

> 259 **pneumothorax** air trapped next to a lung
> 260 ***Al hamdullellah!*** Praise to God
> 262 ***shalwar-kameez*** traditional Islamic dress comprising a long
> top hanging over trousers
> 270 **hodgepodge** mixture

CHAPTER 24

- Amir invites Sohrab to go back to the USA with him.
- Soraya is happy for Amir to bring Sohrab home.
- The process of adoption is difficult and Amir admits to Sohrab that he may have to go into another orphanage for a time.

In Islamabad, Farid finds them a hotel near the Shah Faisal Mosque. Sohrab shows his first sign of interest as they pass the mosque. Having seen them into their room, Farid leaves to return to his family. Sohrab falls asleep on his bed and Amir does likewise. When Amir wakes, the boy is gone. He goes down to the front desk but the manager is unhelpful and says he has not seen Sohrab. However, Amir remembers the boy looking at the mosque and believes he will have gone there. He convinces the hotel manager to take him to the mosque.

Amir finds Sohrab sitting on a patch of grass near the mosque. The manager leaves him there. Amir sits with the boy and they talk about their parents. Amir gives Sohrab the Polaroid of his father to help him remember his face. Sohrab starts to cry and asks if he is going to hell for hurting Assef. Amir asserts that the man he shot has always been bad and that he hurt Hassan and that Hassan would be proud of his son for what he did. Sohrab tells Amir he is glad the people he loved are gone so they cannot see how full of sin he is. He reveals that the Taliban men 'did things' (p. 278) to him which he is ashamed of. He cries and Amir asks him to go back to the USA with him.

They spend a week together, letting Amir recover and getting to know each other. In one conversation Amir reveals to Sohrab that

CONTEXT

The Shah Faisal Mosque is one of the largest mosques in the world. It was built between 1976 and 1986 to a controversial design. It is about 5,000 square meters in area and can hold over a quarter of a million worshippers.

he is his father's brother. He explains that Hassan did not know this because of his heritage, but that Baba loved them both equally. That night they talk again about San Francisco. Sohrab expresses his fear that Amir might not want to keep him, but Amir dismisses it. Sohrab confides in him that he does not want to go to another orphanage and Amir promises never to let that happen.

> **CONTEXT**
>
> The INS was the United States Immigration and Naturalization Service. It was responsible for legal and illegal immigration and naturalisation until it ceased to exist on 1 March 2003. Its functions were taken over by three agencies within the new Department of Homeland Security.

Amir calls Soraya and she agrees to let him adopt Sohrab and bring him back to the USA. Amir takes Sohrab with him to the US embassy to talk about the adoption but he is told there is very little chance that it will be successful because of international adoption laws. He speaks to Soraya again and she informs him that her uncle who works for the INS is going to see what he can do to help the process.

Amir goes to see an immigration lawyer, who also tries to dissuade Amir, advising him that adopting Sohrab and taking him home will be a very difficult thing to achieve. The options he presents are for Amir to live with the boy for two years in Pakistan or to put him into an orphanage and return home to undertake the process from there. Amir returns to the hotel and tells Sohrab that he hopes to be able to take him to the USA but that Sohrab may have to go into an orphanage for a time. He tries to convince the boy that an orphanage in Pakistan would be much nicer than the one in Kabul but the boy is still terrified by the prospect.

That night Amir is woken by a phone call from Soraya. She informs him that the key to adopting Sohrab is just to take him into the USA and then do the paperwork, that the process is much easier when the child is already in place. Amir goes to tell Sohrab, who is in the bathroom, but what he sees there causes him to drop to his knees and start screaming.

COMMENTARY

The mosque Sohrab runs to is a sign of his having been brought up by Hassan as a good Muslim, but also a sign that Sohrab does not associate his fear of the Taliban with the mosque and thinks of it as a safe place. The suggestion is that, for Sohrab, the Taliban are not associated with his religion.

Amir's panic at finding Sohrab missing reflects the fact that this is probably the first time he has had to be truly responsible for someone else. Having closed the previous chapter of his life, this is the sign of a new chapter beginning. When the manager of the hotel agrees to help Amir he says to him it is because he is 'a father like you' (p. 275). Although Amir is not Sohrab's father, this is now the position he finds himself in.

When the manager leaves Amir outside the mosque he says to Amir that 'you people [Afghans] are a little reckless' (p. 275). This causes Amir to laugh. In part this is at the thought of someone as cautious as him being thought reckless, but also because it is now true. He has finally accepted his Afghan identity. The presumption is that Sohrab, like his father, has been raped by Assef and others. Amir is once again presented with a boy to whom something painful has happened, but this time he has the chance to put it right. Rather than ignoring the problem and pushing the boy away, as he did with Hassan, he draws him against his chest and lets the boy cry.

Amir's decision to take Sohrab to the USA with him is the final stage in his change from the Amir who arrived in Pakistan. He has paid his debts and is now ready to be a father. If all the bad things that have happened to him and to Afghanistan can be seen as his punishment for his sins, then now, having repented and been forgiven for them, he receives a reward: the son he has always wanted. Although the path will not be a straightforward one – Amir is forced to admit he might have to break his promise to Sohrab – Amir keeps trying and through Soraya is provided with a simple solution.

QUESTION
Amir is, in general, a non-practising Muslim. However, religion is an important part of the novel. How does religion influence the story?

CHECK THE BOOK
Victor Hugo's novel *Les Misérables* (1862), which is mentioned in this chapter, is also a novel in which much of the **narrative** is driven by the main character seeking redemption for past mistakes.

GLOSSARY	
272	**carafe** glass bottle
276	*masjid* mosque
279	**kinship** feeling of being closely bound together
279	*Pakeeza* Indian film of 1972
282	*Haddith* teachings of the prophet Muhammad
283	*tashweesh* worry
286	**Javert** the name of the police inspector in *Les Misérables*
295	**milieu** environment, living conditions
298	*Rawsti* anyway, after all

CHAPTER 25

- We learn that Sohrab has attempted suicide but has survived.
- Amir takes Sohrab back to the USA, but the boy is now withdrawn and uncommunicative.
- Helping to fly a kite in a kite fight starts the return of Sohrab's spirit.

CHECK THE FILM

In the 2007 film adaptation of *The Kite Runner*, Sohrab's suicide attempt is not included. According to the director's DVD commentary this is due only to restrictions of time.

The action moves to a hospital. The staff will not let Amir be with Sohrab while they treat him. He rushes to a supply room and, taking a white bedsheet to use as a prayer mat, proceeds to pray and cry for both Hassan and his son.

Eventually Amir moves to the waiting room. He cannot settle down to reading because the image of Sohrab in the bath with his wrists cut keeps coming back to him. Sohrab has been in surgery for five hours. Finally, Amir sleeps. He is woken by a doctor who informs him how bad the boy's injuries were, but that Sohrab is alive. Amir cries again, but this time in relief.

Eventually they move Sohrab to a normal bed in another room. Sohrab is awake and Amir talks to him but the boy does not respond. Amir has bought a copy of the storybook which he used to read to Hassan. He reads a little to the boy and when he stops the boy finally speaks but only to say he is 'tired of everything' (p. 308). Sohrab tells Amir that he wants his old life back and that he wishes Amir had left him in the bath to die. Amir says that he now has a visa to take the boy back to the USA. This news doesn't ease Sohrab's depression and Amir informs us that it will be a year before he speaks again.

A week later, Amir takes him home with him. Soraya and Amir are pleased to see each other, but there is little reaction from Sohrab. In the middle of the night Amir finds the Polaroid under the boy's pillow and wonders if Baba thought of Hassan as his true son. He replaces the photograph and notes the absence of painful emotions.

The next day Soraya's parents come to meet the boy. The general asks why his son-in-law has brought this 'Hazara boy' (p. 315) to live with them. Amir reveals the truth about Sohrab's parentage and chastises his father-in-law for his racism.

For months Sohrab is silent and withdrawn. During the same period the events of 9/11 take place and Amir and Soraya become involved in projects to end the years of war and unhappiness in their homeland.

The story comes up to date. Amir is with his wife, his mother-in-law and Sohrab at an Afghan gathering in Fremont Park. It is raining in the park and, as they shelter, they tell jokes and talk turns to Baba. Finally the skies clear and they emerge from shelter. Games are played and, later, kites are flown. Amir buys a kite and takes it to Sohrab. He talks about kites and about how he and Hassan would fly and run for kites. Sohrab shows interest but says nothing and when Amir offers to let him help he does not agree. However, when Amir starts to fly the kite by himself he looks down and Sohrab is there. He hands the spool to the boy and Sohrab takes it then helps him to fight another kite. This process wakes Sohrab from his trance and, as the other kite spins away, Amir sees a smile on his face. In response, Amir runs after the kite for Sohrab.

COMMENTARY

As Amir waits for Sohrab to be treated following his suicide attempt, and during his recovery, the process whereby Sohrab has become fused in his mind with Hassan comes to an end. Amir has now totally accepted Sohrab as his kin, his responsibility, even as his son. He starts to pray, something which has not been important to him for a long time, but which is important to Sohrab. The survival of Sohrab comes immediately after Amir's prayers, suggesting that these prayers have been answered and that there will be a continued reawakening of Amir's faith, a final reconnection with his heritage.

The re-emergence of the storybook signals a return to the **motif** of stories and storytelling, and also shows Amir trying to find a way to connect with the boy. Following the suicide attempt, Amir feels the need to reconnect with Sohrab, but also to apologise to the boy for letting him down. The book is his way to try to achieve this, and in the process it represents a reconnection with Hassan.

> **CONTEXT**
>
> The events of 11 September 2001, when Al Qaeda terrorists hijacked four commercial aeroplanes and crashed two into the twin towers of the World Trade Center and one into the Pentagon in Washington, triggered the NATO-led invasion of Afghanistan and the overthrow of the Taliban.

> **CONTEXT**
>
> In a case of life mirroring art, just as Amir becomes involved in a rebuilding project in Afghanistan, so author Khaled Hosseini urged his publisher to donate money for a primary school in Arababshirali, in northern Afghanistan.

There are signs in this chapter that Amir's journey to find himself is at an end. The first is when he looks at the photograph of Hassan and, instead of the turmoil he expects, finds a peace inside himself. He reflects on his old pain 'gathering its things, packing up, and slipping away unannounced in the middle of the night' (p. 313). The next comes when he stands up to his father-in-law's racist attitude to Sohrab, telling him, in formal adult terms, 'You will never again refer to him as "Hazara boy" in my presence' (p. 315). This is a reaction to the kind of comment that Amir has ignored in the past. Taking a stand against it shows a newfound strength and confidence, similar to that of his father.

CHECK THE POEM

A famous example of **pathetic fallacy** can be found in William Wordsworth's poem, 'I Wandered Lonely as a Cloud' (1807).

Finally, the story returns to its main **motif**, kite flying, with another scene in which the weather – clouds clearing to produce clear, sunny skies – reflects the emotional tone of the scene. Sohrab has been withdrawn since his suicide attempt and his change of location to the USA. However, kite flying, an activity which Hassan shared with both Amir and his son, finally brings them closer together. At the end of the kite fight Amir offers to run the kite for Sohrab, reversing the roles which existed between him and Hassan. As he runs he utters Hassan's phrase 'For you, a thousand times over' (p. 323) and returns to the lyrical prose which he has used to describe the most significant things in his life, showing both his loyalty and his devotion to the boy.

GLOSSARY		
300	**iodine ... peroxide**	chemicals used as antiseptics
300	**gurney**	trolley used for moving patients in a hospital
305	**ICU**	Intensive Care Unit
307	*aush*	stew
313	**epiphany**	sudden realisation
315	**erroneous**	wrong
316	**Hamid Karzai**	Afghan president after 2004
319	*Loya jirga*	grand assembly
319	*morgh kebab*	grilled chicken kebab
320	*seh-parcha*	type of fabric
320	*Sawl-e-nau mubabrak*	Happy New Year
322	*sabagh*	lesson

EXTENDED COMMENTARIES

TEXT 1 – CHAPTER 3, PAGES 12–14

From 'In the late 1960s ...' to '... hating him a little.'

Although we have already been introduced to the characters of Amir, Hassan and Baba in the first two chapters of the novel, this particular part of Chapter 3 lays out clearly the dynamic between the three characters. The relationships that are outlined here define how the characters interact for the rest of the novel.

The passage takes place first at Lake Ghargha, later the scene of Hassan's dream about the hidden monster, and then at Baba's orphanage. Amir, at this point, is narrating his childhood memories of his father and the building of the orphanage in particular. Amir's **narrative** voice is quite simple, almost childlike, reflecting the perspective of his memories: 'He asked me to fetch Hassan too, but I lied and told him Hassan had the runs. I wanted Baba all to myself' (p. 12). As such, the events related make Baba seem larger than life – as they would to a small child – and aid in the process of mythologising Baba, an attitude which seems to form a large part of Amir's stories about his father throughout the novel.

At the beginning of the passage we are told that Baba has designed the orphanage himself despite having no experience. This shows Baba to be a man who knows his own mind, doesn't listen to discouraging advice, and who is stubborn enough to carry on regardless. This is echoed at the end of the passage where we learn that he had the same attitude to both his business dealings and his marriage. However, it is significant, in terms of Baba's relationship with his son, that Amir identifies himself as the one thing his father had not 'molded ... to his liking' (p. 14).

The ability to affect the world around him is a key trait which Amir sees in his father, and many of the anecdotes concerning Baba which Amir relates throughout the novel have this as their main theme. However, the fact that Amir is not malleable in the same way is also always present. During scenes where Baba demonstrates his great abilities, Amir is often shown being unable to live up to his father's wishes.

CHECK THE BOOK

Sebastian Faulks's novel *Birdsong* (1993), although focusing on the First World War, is similar to *The Kite Runner* in that it examines war through both a historical perspective and a more contemporary one and examines the extended consequences of war on people and their relationships.

CHECK THE BOOK

Orphans and orphanages are recurring **motifs** in *The Kite Runner* and in other literature, including Charles Dickens's *Oliver Twist* (1837–8) and Charlotte Brontë's *Jane Eyre* (1847).

In this particular passage, while Baba is making ready to open the orphanage, we are shown a scene of the two of them having a picnic at the lake. Amir describes himself asking childish questions and making seemingly random comments about having cancer. This extreme opposition of their behaviour creates a barrier between Amir and Baba: one of the threads running through the novel is Amir's attempts to remove this barrier.

Hassan is not included in the scene which Amir relates, but it is his absence which is key to this passage. Baba has suggested bringing Hassan along with them on their picnic, but Amir has lied to prevent Hassan from coming. Seeing the affection which Baba has for Hassan is hurtful to Amir, and this leads to the cruelty which Amir sometimes shows towards Hassan. This cruelty, submerged in Amir's personality, would seem to be the 'monster' that Hassan later dreams inhabits this lake. However, by preventing Hassan from coming to the lake, Amir can avoid the guilt which he always feels about these cruel episodes. This acts as a **foreshadowing** of Amir driving Hassan away after his rape.

The passage then moves on to the day of the opening of the orphanage and we see Baba once again as an idealised figure. However, as well as Amir's larger-than-life portrayal of his father, we also see other people's reactions to him. This allows us to understand that Baba's charisma and abilities are real rather than simply the romanticised views of his son.

This scene also shows us how proud Amir is of his father. For all that there may be a barrier between the two of them caused by Amir having a very different personality from his father, Amir still wishes to emulate Baba. This contradiction is what powers Amir's story and his journey towards reconciliation with his father.

During this scene there is a moment when Baba's hat blows off and Amir is asked to hold it for him. The **symbolism** of this moment suggests a self-sufficiency in Baba – he can carry on his speech without needing the support of his hat – and Amir's need to cling on to his father. It also suggests a transference from Baba to Amir: an element of Baba attempting to pass his stature and gravitas to his son. However, Amir is not ready to accept this gift, he can only

hold the hat. He is not yet ready to wear it. This is emphasised by
the fact that the people who come up to congratulate his father
tousle Amir's hair – a symbol of his immaturity and of not yet being
ready to assume the mantle of his father. The question that this
passage therefore poses is: will he ever be ready?

TEXT 2 – CHAPTER 7, PAGES 67–9

From 'I stopped watching ...' to ' ... And that was good.'

This passage contains the pivotal events of the novel. These events
are the subject of the foreshadowing which has been occurring in
previous chapters. They are frequently referenced in later chapters
as the source of Amir's guilt and the driving force behind his desire
to redeem himself.

The passage opens with Amir looking away from the rape of
Hassan which is occurring in the alley. The movement of the
character is mirrored in the way the passage is written. Although it
is clear enough to inform the reader of what is happening, it
describes the actual attack obliquely, using the sounds and Amir's
imaginings and emotions, rather than a graphic description of the
rape. Amir tells us that he is 'biting down on my first, hard enough
to draw blood from the knuckles [and] weeping' (p. 67). Amir's
blood and tears mirror the blood and tears that would be coming
from Hassan at the same time but, by focusing on Amir, Hosseini
provides an impression of the pain and horror of what is occurring
without it being too literal.

Amir then describes his pivotal moment: the decision whether to
step into the alley and do something to help his friend, or to run
away. He chooses to run away, and the suggestion is that he does not
stop running until the end of the novel when he finally makes up for
taking the wrong decision at this crucial moment.

The fact that the events are occurring in an alley is symbolic of their
hidden and dark nature. Amir's failure to enter the alley shows his
inability and unwillingness to deal with the darker side of life and
highlights the protected nature of his upbringing up to this point.
When he runs away, Amir runs to the bazaar, an open and very

> **? QUESTION**
> This scene
> has been alluded
> to many times
> before we actually
> reach it. What
> effect does this
> have on our
> ultimate reception
> of it?

public space, taking refuge in a place which represents the safety and shelter which he is used to.

As he runs, Amir tries to rationalise his decision. At first he explains that 'I ran because I was a coward' (p. 68). Then he tries to convince himself that it is not cowardice but self-interest which drives him, and that sacrificing Hassan to placate Assef is the price he has had to pay in order to win Baba's approval: a balancing of fortune for winning the kite fight. This is not a rational thought, based as it is in a superstitious belief, but it shows how Amir's treatment of Hassan is tied up so closely with his desire to gain his father's love. He finishes this thought by dismissing Hassan: 'He was just a Hazara, wasn't he?' (p. 68). This is not typical of Amir who is usually much more open minded about Hassan's ethnicity than the people around him, but it shows not only how ingrained the racism is in the culture, but how much of his own personal belief Amir is willing to set aside in the search for reconciliation with his father.

It is worth remembering at this point that this is not necessarily a true picture of Amir's thoughts at the time because they are being related to us as part of the adult Amir's recollections of the event. As this is the moment that he himself has identified as the crucial event in his life it is bound to be coloured by the subsequent thirty years of guilt and constantly running over the event in his mind. As such, the self-recrimination that runs through this passage is largely that of the adult, not of the child.

CHECK THE BOOK

In the story 'An Encounter' in his collection *Dubliners* (1914), James Joyce also describes a disturbing scene through a voice which is part child and part adult.

Hassan emerges from the alley and Amir confronts him. As he does so he takes a cruel attitude towards him rather than offering care or comfort, asking, 'Where were you? I looked for you?' (p. 68). This anger would seem to be Amir's reaction to his guilt and an extension of the cruelty he has shown to Hassan from an early age.

At the end of the passage (and chapter), Amir returns home with the precious kite and is greeted by his father with the affection and love for which Amir has been searching: 'It happened just the way I'd imagined' (p. 69). It would seem that his bargain to exchange Hassan for his father's good regard has come to fruition. Amir is able, for the time of his father's hug, to forget what he has done. However, we know from the preceding dialogue that this moment of respite will be short and the events in that alley will haunt him for many years. As such, we can already see how the gaining of his father's affection will soon be tainted by the bargain which Amir has made to attain it.

TEXT 3 – CHAPTER 19, PAGES 203–4

From 'We had crossed the border ...' to '... alongside the road.'

This passage does two things. It gives us a shorthand description of the state of Afghanistan at the time of Amir's visit, and it also emphasises the great extent to which Amir's need to re-engage with his nationality and ethnicity form part of his journey.

The first paragraph gives us a description of what Amir sees from his car window. In doing so he echoes the strongly **imagistic** language which has been used elsewhere to describe the significant things in his life. In this case, the images are turned towards the destruction and desolation of the country, making the description all the more effective. As well as describing the current state of Afghanistan, it also deals with the history which has brought the country to its current state. First we are shown the poor housing, much of which is seemingly uninhabitable, damaged by fighting. Nearby there are children 'dressed in rags' (p. 203). The people are living in extreme poverty: their houses destroyed and their clothing in tatters.

The next image is of a group of men sitting on 'an old burned-out Soviet-tank' (p. 203). This brings in the Soviet invasion and the wars of the late 1970s and 1980s. However, because we are told that the tank is now only a relic, we know that this is just another part of the story which has led to the scenes of poverty and devastation. Behind the men is a woman dressed in a burqa. This is a specifically Islamic garment which covers the woman's entire body and, in Afghanistan, all of the face except the eyes. The fact that the woman is wearing this particular item represents the regime of the Taliban and their oppression of the Afghan people, the completion of the story which Amir sees from his car window.

CHECK THE BOOK

In his second novel, *A Thousand Splendid Suns* (2007), Hosseini explores the experience of wearing a burqa.

CHECK THE POEM
The term 'tourist' is often used to indicate a voyeur who watches without taking part or taking responsibility. Paul Engle explores this idea in his poem entitled 'Tourist' from his collection *A Woman Unashamed and Other Poems* (1965).

Amir's reaction to these sights is to express his feeling of alienation from his country and his people by comparing himself to a visitor. He says to Farid, 'I feel like a tourist in my own country' (p. 203). The use of the word 'tourist' shows the extent of the distance he feels, because a tourist is a person who visits places for fun and generally has no interaction with the indigenous people, as opposed to a traveller or other type of visitor. Farid picks up on this word and accuses Amir of having always been a tourist in Afghanistan. He goes on to surmise a background for Amir which is remarkably close to the truth and lays bare just how protected Amir has always been from the realities of life in Afghanistan. This confirms that the picture Amir has painted of the Afghanistan of his youth was of a privileged family, rather than a typical one. The suggestion is that Amir has never really understood what it means to be an Afghan because he has been insulated from the reality by his father.

Farid's reaction to Amir in this passage is not representative of the welcome which Amir receives in his home country and is in sharp contrast to the attitude of Wahid, Farid's brother, later in the chapter. However, it would seem to represent the underlying thoughts of at least some of the Afghans who remained behind during the troubles, and suggests that a greater level of cynicism has become standard in the ordinary citizens.

Amir reacts to Farid's verbal attack with a bout of car sickness. This is once again a sign of his weakness and inability to cope with the pressures of life. It is a measure of how unlike his father he is. However, coming hard on the heels of the revelation regarding Amir's protected status, it suggests that his weakness is a reaction to his having been overprotected. At the points when the real world impinges on him, Amir becomes ill. Facing this will be the final step on Amir's journey to maturity.

PART THREE

CRITICAL APROACHES

CHARACTERISATION

Although *The Kite Runner* is a novel which examines the turbulent history of Afghanistan between 1970 and 2001, it is also a novel that particularly focuses on its characters and the relationships between them. In this respect, despite the sometimes experimental nature of its **narrative** structure, and the fact that it is often credited as the first English-language novel written by an Afghan, it is often credited as very much a traditional novel, similar in nature to those by Dickens or Austen. Amir is the main character but also the **narrator**. As the person through whose perspective we see all the other characters, the novel relies on him securing our sympathies so that we are led to care about the others.

The other main characters include Hassan, the 'kite runner' of the title, and Baba, Amir's father. It is the examination of Amir's love for these characters which creates any affection that we as readers hold for them and which drives the story. We have only Amir's perspective to rely on in our understanding of the story and, at times, he does or says things which might undermine our trust of his narration, such as his attempts to justify his actions towards Hassan, or his sometimes exaggerated descriptions of his father's greatness. In this respect we should bear in mind that we are receiving a partial account of events from a single perspective and that our view of the characters is always seen through Amir's interpretations of them.

The only other evidence we receive about the nature of the characters in the novel comes from letters which Amir receives and one chapter which is entirely devoted to a story being told by Rahim Khan. As well as providing vital narrative information and giving us a sense of the individual voices of these other characters, these interludes give us a measure to judge our level of trust in the narrator.

CHECK THE BOOK

The Kite Runner is largely a novel about men and their relationships in the absence of women. As a counterbalance to this, Hosseini's second novel, *A Thousand Splendid Suns* (2007), concentrates on the experience of women in Afghanistan over the same time period.

**CHECK
THE BOOK**

E. L. Konigsburg's
*The View from
Saturday* (1996) is
another novel
which uses
flashback to tell the
story and has
interjections from
other narrators in
the first person.
Although aimed at
a much younger
audience than *The
Kite Runner*, it has a
similar moral about
kindness and
friendship versus
cruelty and
selfishness.

**CHECK
THE FILM**

In the novel we are
never provided with
a second name for
Amir or the rest of
his family. However,
in order to provide
copies of Amir's
novel as props in
the film, Khaled
Hosseini was asked
to invent a surname
for the character,
making him Amir
Qadiri. Qadiri is the
name of an Islamic
religious order.

AMIR

Amir is the main character and the **narrator** of the story. The whole story is told by him during a period between December 2001 and March 2002 but covers events in Amir's life from his childhood in the early 1970s up to his present. Unlike other characters, we are never given a description of Amir, so our picture of him must be inferred from his voice.

The young Amir lives in an Afghanistan which has been at relative peace for decades and is a stable environment, different from the country of the early twenty-first century. This allows Amir to present himself as a happy and settled child who enjoys his life and his friendship with Hassan, the Hazara boy who is also his servant.

Quite near the beginning of the novel he tells us 'I never thought of Hassan and me as friends' (p. 22), suggesting that he felt distanced from Hassan, probably due to their different ethnicity and statuses in life. However, this is an early sign that we cannot always rely on the things Amir chooses to tell us because it is clear from the tales he relates that Hassan was indeed his closest friend. The desire to distance himself from the boy is a result of his childhood jealousy and also of his later guilt colouring earlier events.

The major influence in Amir's life is, of course, Hassan himself. Although they are only friends for the first thirteen years of Amir's life, it is clear that this is the defining relationship in his life. This can be inferred from the fact that the novel itself is named after Hassan, but also from the way in which every event that Amir relates ties back to the other boy, either in terms of their great friendship, or in terms of Amir's guilt over his betrayal of that friendship, such as on his wedding day when he wonders if Hassan has married and 'whose face he had seen in the mirror under the veil' (p. 149). Even at such an intimate moment, his thoughts turn to Hassan.

Amir tells us himself in the opening line of the novel that the person he is was formed on the day in the alley in 1975. Although we don't find out for another five chapters what this event was, everything we are told, both before and after the revelation, is tinged with the emotions of anger, guilt and sorrow emerging from it.

CHARACTERISATION

However, as well as being a burden, his feelings about Hassan are also a positive force in Amir's life. His desire to write is formed by his time spent reading stories to Hassan. His later success as a writer can be seen to emerge from a desire to assuage his guilt by doing something which he knows Hassan would enjoy and approve of, thanks to the stories they shared as children. Also, his marriage to Soraya and his yearning for children can be seen as his way of recreating the situation of his own childhood but this time with the chance to make up for his past mistakes. This idea is even more powerfully emphasised when the story moves to modern-day Kabul at the end of the novel. When Rahim Khan asks Amir to save Sohrab, Amir is really being given a second chance to save his friend.

One blot on Amir's early life is the lack of love and respect which he feels he gets from his father. The first half of the novel concerns the tensions which Amir feels in his life between wanting to be his own man and the desire to be the man his father wants him to be. This is also a central factor, so he tells us, in his decision not to help Hassan during the attack in the alley.

After Baba's death, although he no longer features as a character in the events being related, he is still a presence in Amir's life, and Amir's decision to revisit Kabul and to retrieve Sohrab can be seen as his attempt to finally reconcile his feelings for his father. By standing up to Assef and literally fighting for possession of Sohrab, who is Baba's grandson, Amir finds a way to become the man his father wanted him to be. This is demonstrated further upon his return to the USA when he becomes involved in building a hospital in Afghanistan in a direct reflection of his father building the orphanage.

Another main strand of Amir's life, and one which runs contrary to his father's wishes, is his interest in stories and writing. This is an inherited trait from his mother who was a teacher of literature. It also provides an escape, first from the perceived lack of love from his father, and later from having to acknowledge the problems in his life and in his homeland. Writing is seen as a retreat and it is telling that, upon his return to Afghanistan, he admits that he is not currently writing about the country. Instead he has written most recently about 'a university professor who joins a clan of gypsies

> **CONTEXT**
>
> 'The setting in 1970s Kabul, the house where Amir lived, the films that he watches, of course the kite flying, the love of storytelling – all of that is from my own childhood. The story line is fictional' (Khaled Hosseini, interview with Erika Milvy on **www.salon.com**).

after he finds his wife in bed with one of his students' (p. 206). Thinking about this book in the context of his current location he continues, 'But suddenly I was embarrassed by it. I hoped Wahid wouldn't ask what it was about' (p. 206).

The Kite Runner can be seen as Amir's attempt to write a book about Afghanistan, and in doing so to place himself back in context. In order to cope with his various anxieties and find a way to understand them Amir makes his life into a **narrative**. In this way, *The Kite Runner* can be seen as an act of catharsis as Amir attempts to make sense of his various actions and emotions by arranging them into a coherent story.

HASSAN

As the 'kite runner' of the title, Hassan is arguably the most significant character in the novel. While Amir is the **narrator**, and the novel is the relating of his story, Hassan's story and what he represents to Amir, and to Baba, are the crucial driving forces in the novel. This is all the more remarkable in that he disappears from Amir's story relatively early on, and reappears only in Rahim Khan's story and one posthumous letter. As such, he exists in most of the novel as a presence, looming over the narrative, rather than as a character taking parts in events.

We are presented with a very clear physical description of Hassan in Chapter 2, including his 'flat broad nose and slanting, narrow eyes like bamboo leaves' (p. 3), his 'tiny low-set ears and ... pointed stub of a chin' (p. 3) and the cleft lip which is corrected in Chapter 5. However, as mentioned above, all that we learn about Hassan, apart from the one letter with which we are presented in Chapter 17, comes via Amir's perception of him. What we are told is therefore a partial perspective on Hassan. The portrait which Amir paints is of a boy much more at ease with himself and his place in the world than Amir himself, and than we might be led to expect from his situation. Hassan has been born into servitude but does not seem to resent this. He is also burdened with an ill father and the fact that, as an Hazara, he lives in a country which looks down on his ethnic group. However, he receives a great deal of warmth and love from

CONTEXT

'[H]e [Amir] is a better **protagonist** for a novel ... than Hassan, who is so firmly rooted in goodness and integrity. There was a lot more room for character development with Amir than Hassan' (Khaled Hosseini, interview with Farhad Azad on www.afghan magazine.com, June 2004).

Ali and so does not suffer from the same need to strive for his father's affections which is a feature of so much of Amir's life.

Up to the point of the rape, the hardships with which Hassan has to live do not seem to bother him very much. This may be a true picture of the young servant, however we must remember that the tales of Hassan are coloured by thirty years of Amir's guilt. As a consequence of this guilt, Amir feels the need to remember his friend as happy and carefree up to the point of his betrayal. Due to Amir's self-editing, the only way to get a true impression of Hassan is by reading through Amir's description to reveal the truth of Hassan's early life, and also from the letter Hassan writes to Amir twenty-five years after they last see each other.

For example, it is clear that Hassan has been forced to grow up faster than Amir. For all that Hassan is physically a year younger than Amir, at times he acts more like an adult. In Chapter 6, he is happy to let Amir win at cards, knowing that to do otherwise might provoke an outburst. During this game, Amir offers, when they have grown up, to buy him a television and Hassan replies, 'I'll put it on my table, where I keep my drawings' (p. 51). This comment makes Amir sad because it shows that Hassan believes his life will never change, never improve, and that he will always live in the same hut he currently shares with his father.

> **? QUESTION**
> How would the novel be different if Hassan had been the narrator?

There is also the resignation with which he greets both Amir's question about eating dirt and the pomegranate attack. The willingness to take whatever is forced upon him shows a child who is used to carrying burdens and coming off second best; who is willing to take responsibility for Amir's actions without comment. This comparison can be extended in the way Hassan responds to Amir's enquiry about eating dirt in simple, non-judgemental tones – 'Would you ever ask me to do such a thing, Amir agha?' (p. 48) – and later, during the pomegranate attack, by literally turning his cheek.

The only time we are presented with Hassan's direct voice, rather than it being filtered through Amir's perceptions, is in the letter he gives to Rahim Khan to pass to Amir. This is an adult Hassan, not the child of Amir's recollections, but the contents of the letter throw light on the character of Hassan as he must have been, even as a child. He opens and closes the letter with religious invocations. While Amir has mentioned Hassan's beliefs, they are obviously of greater importance to Hassan than we might assume from Amir's tales. The letter continues with a kind and considerate tone, using phrases such as 'I pray that this letter finds you in good health' (p. 189). It is clear that Hassan does not hold a grudge against Amir for his past actions and he is not weighed down by those actions as Amir is. In this respect, it shows Amir's guilt to be a one-sided and selfish emotion and to have caused more damage to both children than the rape itself. It is only when he allows himself to comfort Sohrab following the revelation of his molestation by Assef and the other Taliban that Amir finally understands what Hassan had suffered and how he, Amir, should have dealt with it. Hassan signs off his letter by referring to himself as Amir's friend, something which Amir could never bring himself to do. It shows us that Hassan's love and loyalty to his former master have not waned over the years.

BABA

Baba is Amir's father. Once again what we learn about him is mostly shown via Amir's perspective. Amir is very proud of his father and somewhat in awe of him. As such Baba is often painted as a larger-than-life character who is almost unbelievably charismatic and successful. Amir describes him as 'a towering Pashtun specimen with a thick beard, a wayward crop of curly brown hair [and] hands that looked capable of uprooting a willow tree' (p. 11). Given the way Amir sees his father it would be easy to assume that this is an overstatement. However, as corroboration, Amir adds a quotation from Rahim Khan that Baba had a 'black glare that would "drop the devil to his knees begging for mercy"' (p. 11).

> **CONTEXT**
>
> Although we are not given another name for him, Baba is actually the Arabic word for 'father'.

By interpreting what Amir says about his father and looking at the ways in which other people are reported to act around him we can ultimately put together an understanding of his character. From the reactions of the man who kisses Baba's hand after Baba prevents the Russian soldier from raping his wife, and the men in the bar in Hayward who become friends and admirers of Baba in a single evening after Amir's graduation, it is clear that, unless Amir's account of his father is entirely fictitious, Baba has a powerfully charismatic personality which affects the people around him.

It is certain that Baba is a successful man. He lives in a large house, which he himself built, in a wealthy and respectable part of Kabul. We know this last fact not merely from Amir's reports but from the fact that under the rule of the Taliban the elite of Afghanistan's regime choose to live in that area, and in that house in particular. In addition the building of an orphanage is the act of a wealthy man. It is also, however, the act of a concerned member of society, a benefactor and a man with a love of children. This is not always a side of Baba which Amir reveals – in large part due to his own feelings of alienation from his father's love.

The story which Amir tells of his father wrestling with a black bear gives us an example of the high regard in which Amir holds his father. It is the kind of story which seems more like a myth or a fable than a true anecdote and suggests that Amir's regard is almost a form of worship of his father as some kind of god or idol. Indeed, Amir tells us that he dreams about his father wrestling with the bear, and that 'in those dreams I can never tell Baba from the bear' (p. 11).

One key to Baba's inner character is the loss of his wife, Sofia, at the moment of Amir's birth. Amir believes that Baba hates him for causing Sofia's death. While this is probably largely untrue and is, in fact, another product of Amir's guilt and poor self-esteem, it is certain that this loss affected his father. Baba does not remarry, nor are we told of any other women in his life, other than his affair with Sanaubar, so we can assume that he still thinks of her as his wife and does not want to replace her. With regard to the influence of this on his relationship with Amir, it is doubtful that he blames his son for her death, but it is likely that Amir reminds Baba of Sofia with his love of books and reading that comes from his mother. This would account, to some extent, for the distance that Amir feels between him and his father. Baba can allow himself to feel closer to his other son, Hassan, because there is not the same set of associations.

A second key to Baba's character comes once we learn that he is Hassan's father. This sheds light on his actions all the way through

CHECK THE BOOK

Oil (1927), by Upton Sinclair, which was made into the 2007 film *There Will Be Blood,* also concerns a son who struggles to live up to his father's expectations.

the novel. Part of Amir's alienation from his father comes from the way that he insists on treating Hassan equally to him. Only when Amir realises that Hassan was actually his half-brother can he come to see this as fair, rather than an insult whereby he is seen to be of no more importance to his father than the servant's son.

Baba's need to overcome his guilt over his affair with Sanaubar, and his torment at his inability to publicly name Hassan as his son, in many ways make him the driven and proud man who is presented to us through Amir's **narrative**.

ALI

Ali is Hassan's father and a childhood friend of Baba. His relationship with Amir's father is a direct reflection of Hassan's relationship with Amir. Left as an orphan at a young age, Ali was brought up by Baba's father's servants and was a servant to Baba in the same way that Hassan was brought up as a servant to Amir.

Having suffered from polio as a child Ali has one withered leg and walks with a profound limp. This makes him an object of fun for the neighbourhood children who are happy to tease and bully him. As with Hassan he also carries the stigma of being an Hazara. We are told that 'Of all the neighborhood boys who tortured Ali, Assef was by far the most relentless' (p. 34). It is, to some extent, the fact of who his father is that leads to Hassan being a target of Assef and his friends.

Although we later find out that Hassan is not his son, Ali does not seem upset by this and treats Hassan with all the love and respect that we can imagine he would have given his biological son. This shows a man who is kind and compassionate as well as loyal. This last aspect is emphasised when Ali and Hassan have to leave Baba's house. Ali obviously knows what Amir has done, and also what he has failed to do, but does not reveal these things to Baba. Hassan has sworn him to secrecy and, even though revealing all to Baba would allow them to stay, and would give Ali a way to get back at Baba for his affair with Sanaubar, Ali keeps his promise to Hassan, and says nothing. This shows that Ali, although mostly in the background of the story, is a man of strong character, and much more of an equal to Baba than Amir is to Hassan.

CONTEXT

Ali's name is symbolic of his ethnicity as an Hazara and his religious leanings as a Shi'a rather than a Sunni Muslim. The Shi'as believe that Ali (the brother-in-law of Muhammad) was the true inheritor of the Islamic faith.

RAHIM KHAN

Rahim Khan is Baba's friend and business colleague. He is a constant presence in Amir's childhood. Where Baba is portrayed as powerful and sometimes dismissive of Amir, Rahim Khan is shown to be sensitive and patient, and as such provides a balance for Baba. He acts as a surrogate parent for Amir, providing the support, guidance and understanding that he fails to get from his father, and can't get from his mother because of her absence. Rahim Khan is a positive influence on Amir and gives him the foundations for his later success.

Rahim Khan reappears later in the novel, but this time as a figure of redemption. Having been such a strong presence in Amir's childhood, he is one of the few people who could cause him to come back to Afghanistan and force him to face his childhood fears and mistakes. As such, having guided Amir through his childhood, he now acts as his guide into adulthood and maturity.

SORAYA

Soraya is Amir's wife and the daughter of an Afghan general. Amir describes her in a series of vivid images which reflect his feelings for her. From his first impressions of 'the way her luminous eyes had fleetingly held mine' (p. 124), to the moments of their wedding when 'A blush, red like henna, bloomed on her cheeks' (p. 149) to the way, upon his return to the USA, he 'smelled apples in her hair' (p. 312), Amir reserves his most colourful and poetic **imagery** for his descriptions of his wife.

She is similar to Amir's mother in that she is a teacher but, like Amir, she has her own guilty past which lays a burden on her (see Chapter 12). Unlike Amir she is able to give up her burden and move on with her life. As such she acts as a reflection of Amir's inability to do these things.

The implication in the text is that the infertility that Soraya and Amir suffer from is Soraya's rather than Amir's, especially as Amir tells us that he passed his fertility test 'with flying colours' (p. 161). However, it would seem, in **metaphorical** terms, that the infertility results from Amir's failure to fully grow up and to move away from

> **CONTEXT**
>
> The name Rahim means 'compassionate', a title which elegantly sums up the role Rahim Khan plays in Amir's life.

> **CONTEXT**
>
> The name Soraya means 'princess' just as the name Amir means 'prince'.

 CHECK THE BOOK

In *Pride and Prejudice* (1813) by Jane Austen, sixteen-year-old Lydia Bennet runs away with a soldier, Mr Wickham. In order to save the family honour, Wickham is paid to marry her.

his childhood. It is only at the end of the story that he appears to earn the gift of a child. This part of the story reflects the history of Ali, Baba and Hassan. Just as Ali was unable to father a child and was given Hassan by Baba, so Amir and Soraya are given Sohrab courtesy of Hassan.

Soraya was the name of the wife of King Amanullah Khan, the reforming king of Afghanistan who was the first ruler of the country following the final Anglo-Afghan war. By using her name, Hosseini connects the story back to a more hopeful and peaceful time in Afghanistan's history.

ASSEF

Assef is Amir's childhood bully and, later, a high-ranking member of the Taliban in Afghanistan. By inhabiting both these roles we are shown how the treatment of the Afghan people by the Taliban is really a form of bullying itself, but on a larger and more comprehensively violent scale. However, the fact that he wears Western-style sunglasses and has a sexual preference for children indicates that he does not hold to the strict moral and religious code that the Taliban espouse and that he is simply using them as a cover to follow his own twisted agenda.

Amir describes Assef as a 'sociopath'. This means he has no regard for the rights or feelings of others or of laws, and is happy to violate those rights and laws without regard to the consequences. By placing Assef at the centre of the most violent and disturbing parts of the novel – bullying, rape, mass murder, execution, etc. – we see how the problems in Afghanistan over the time period covered by the novel are also a result of the pervasive violation of rights and laws by and against many different groups. One group which is particularly victimised is the Hazaras, and Assef's relationships with both Ali and Hassan are representative of this.

Assef's professed love of Hitler is also a significant element of his character. This tells us immediately about his extreme views and instability and provides a short-hand way of understanding his intentions and beliefs.

CHECK THE BOOK

A sociopath is someone who does not have any concern for the normal moral rules of society or the effects their actions have on others. This kind of character is popular with thriller writers, resulting in characters such as Hannibal Lecter in Thomas Harris's *The Silence of the Lambs* (1988).

SOHRAB

Sohrab continues a dynasty of discarded children, starting with Ali who was made an orphan at an early age, moving down through Hassan who was both illegitimate and abandoned by his mother, and finally to Sohrab who is also orphaned. As such these three characters are representative of their ethnic group, the Hazaras, who could be said to be orphaned and abandoned by the Afghan state. If this **metaphor** is continued, however, then the rescue of Sohrab by Amir, an ethnic Pashtun, suggests a potentially positive future for the remaining Hazaras, with a reconciliation and drawing back into the mainstream.

Sohrab is, at least in Amir's eyes, a substitute for Hassan. By saving the boy from the orphanage he is finally able to make up for not saving Hassan from the rape in the alley. The boy himself does not, however, have the same resigned attitude as his father and, when pressed, takes a stand against further brutality by attempting to take his own life. This in large part can be seen as the result of the more traumatic upbringing he has had, with constant violence in Kabul, the death of his parents, and his abuse at the hands of the Taliban.

SOFIA AND SANAUBAR

Sofia and Sanaubar are the absent mothers of Amir and Hassan. Sofia, a teacher at the university, died while giving birth to Amir. As such she is absent in his life but present through his love of books, reading and writing. Because of her untimely death she becomes a **symbol** for both Amir and Baba of things that are good and pure. When Amir later meets a beggar in the devastated Kabul who knew his mother, this is a sign that a memory of goodness can prevail even through the hardest of times.

Amir also carries guilt over the death of his mother, believing that the distance he feels between himself and his father is due to Baba blaming him for her death. It is not stated in the novel, but it would seem reasonable that when he finds out that the cause of this distance between them is, in fact, the illegitimacy of Hassan, Amir would be able to reconcile this aspect of his guilt.

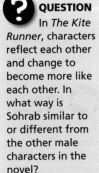

QUESTION
In *The Kite Runner*, characters reflect each other and change to become more like each other. In what way is Sohrab similar to or different from the other male characters in the novel?

CONTEXT
The name Sofia means 'wisdom'.

Sanaubar, in contrast to Sofia, is depicted in very earthy terms as a sexy and sexually active woman who Amir describes as a 'beautiful but notoriously unscrupulous woman who lived up to her dishonourable reputation' (p. 7). Unlike her counterpart, she did not die, but instead deserted Hassan shortly after his birth. Again, this in part can be explained by her unfaithfulness to Ali with Baba. Many years later she returns and we see from Hassan's reaction that he has felt great resentment at her betrayal. However, true to his character, he forgives her and she is welcomed back into the family, becoming a beloved grandmother to Sohrab.

THEMES

FATHERS AND SONS

The Kite Runner is a novel which, in part, examines the relationships between men in the absence of women. In particular it is a novel about fathers and their sons.

CHECK THE BOOK

The relationship between fathers and sons is a common one in literature and a popular topic in Shakespeare's plays, most notably in *Hamlet*, where Hamlet discovers that his uncle has killed his father.

The most prominent example of this theme is the relationship between Baba and Amir. It is a problematic relationship in that Baba has mixed feelings about Amir, both because of Sofia's death and because of his fathering of Hassan. While Amir is unaware of the second of these reasons it is clear to him that his father is not as warm to him as he would like. His attempts to close the distance between them has a great influence on Amir, his personality and the events of his life.

This relationship is finally reconciled on Baba's part when he sees his son grow into a man with a wife. This is made clear when Amir catches Soraya reading his stories to his father. Baba says, 'I put her up to it. I hope you don't mind' (p. 151). Not only is he admitting to the fact that he wanted to hear the stories that he had previously dismissed, but he seeks his son's forgiveness, an act of respect that we have not seen before.

Baba is, of course, also Hassan's father. However, this relationship is never acknowledged and therefore is never reconciled. Hassan has a very positive relationship with Baba who treats him equally with

Amir and does not have to cope with any of the possible animosity or guilt he might feel if Hassan knew his true parentage. Conversely, Baba always carries the guilt both over his betrayal of Ali, but also over the fact that he can never formally acknowledge his other son.

Ali fulfils the role of father for Hassan. He, too, carries the secret of Hassan's parentage, but as he is able to pretend that Hassan is actually his son, it does not seem to affect him in the same way as Baba. Certainly, from Amir's descriptions, it seems that Ali has a closer relationship with Hassan than the one between Baba and Amir.

Another pairing of father and son comes in the form of Hassan and Sohrab. Their lives and relationship are very similar to the relationship between Ali and Hassan, but with the added fact that Hassan is Sohrab's natural father. However, as the novel comes to a close, Amir has replaced Hassan as Sohrab's guardian. This provides a reflection of Ali raising Baba's son as Amir now raises Hassan's, suggesting that the acts of caring, loving and guiding are as influential as blood ties.

CHECK THE POEM
'The child is father of the man' is a line from the poem 'My Heart Leaps Up When I Behold' (1802) by William Wordsworth. It means that our childhood experiences shape the adult we grow up to be. This is particularly true of Amir.

Rahim Khan is also a father figure: he acts as a surrogate father to Amir. When the relationship between Amir and Baba is strained, Rahim Khan provides a source of support and comfort. In his later role, providing Amir with a chance to make amends, he does and says things that Baba may have wished to without ever being able to, and finds a way for Amir to reconcile both himself and Hassan with their father. In his letter he tells Amir, 'I want you to understand that good, real good, was born out of your father's remorse' (p. 263), and goes on to detail some of Baba's actions, such as building the orphanage, feeding the poor, helping friends. Through this we understand that the actions which had made Baba such a legend in Amir's eyes were driven in large part by his remorse over Hassan's parentage. This will allow Amir to equate his own guilt with his father's and therefore feel closer to him.

REDEMPTION

A major theme in the novel is the search for redemption. Amir's story is encapsulated in the offer made to him by Rahim Khan in

CHECK THE POEM

Redemption is a key message of the teachings of Christianity as reflected in much religious poetry, such as 'Redemption' in a collection by Frederick William Orde Ward (published 1916), a poem which promises that however much pain is suffered in life, the power of redemption will heal it.

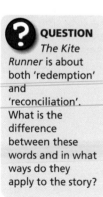

QUESTION

The Kite Runner is about both 'redemption' and 'reconciliation'. What is the difference between these words and in what ways do they apply to the story?

the opening chapter, 'There is a way to be good again' (p. 2). It is the desire to make up for the events of his childhood, and the fear of what it might cost him to achieve this, which drive all of Amir's decisions in the novel and form the basis for his character.

His return to Afghanistan is a key part of this search for redemption, because by going to the USA – and fitting in so well there – he has effectively run away from the events of his childhood, and also from his heritage and all the things which should form the person he is. Only by returning can he reconcile the person he is with the person he wants to be. He returns and rescues Sohrab from the Taliban and, in doing so, symbolically rescues Hassan from his tormentors, thus finally making up for his lack of action all those years ago.

Amir is not the only character searching for redemption, however. His father, both in public activities such as building an orphanage and in the private ways in which he interacts with his two sons, is searching for a way to atone for his infidelity with Sanaubar and his inability to acknowledge Hassan. In addition, in a reaction against this guilt, he feels a need to reconcile his relationship with Amir. While he never gets a chance to resolve his remorse over Ali and Hassan, he and Amir become much closer during their time in the USA.

Soraya is also seeking for redemption for past sins. This is one reason why she and Amir would seem to be such a good match. He is in a position to understand her need for forgiveness and is therefore able, when she informs him of her disgrace, to reply 'Nothing you said changes anything. I want us to marry' (p. 144). Later, when he finds out more details, he once more dismisses the topic, adding 'Let's never talk about this again' (p. 157).

Rahim Khan is also seeking redemption. He carries guilt over his failure to speak up at a time when it could have made a difference, regarding both Hassan's rape and his parentage. Unable to seek atonement for himself, his request that Amir rescues Sohrab from Kabul is his way of achieving this redemption.

RELIGION AND ETHNICITY

Amir, like his father, is not a devout Muslim. The only times he reverts to prayer are during moments of extreme fear and distress. However, both his nominal religion and, especially, his ethnicity form key parts of the narrative for him, as they do for all the other characters.

Although Amir's is mostly a journey of redemption, this is closely tied in with the idea of what it means to be an Afghan. Part of the problem in Amir's relationship with his father results from Baba's idea of what a man should be like, involving his idea of what an Afghan should be like. Baba considers himself an Afghan, no matter the situation, and this is what informs both his bravery in the face of the Russian soldier, and also his anger and confusion when asked for identification in the American mini-market. His ethnicity is an integral part of him and so, when Amir does not match up to his ideal image of what it means to be an Afghan man, this drives the two of them still further apart.

The suggestion of Amir not fitting in as an Afghan is reinforced by the ease with which he slots into American society. This is partly shown by the passages in which he tells us of his studies in the USA, his house and his success as a writer. But it is also clear from how out of place he feels upon his return to Afghanistan. Amir tells Farid that he feels like a tourist in his own country. When Farid replies that Amir has always been a tourist, this simply confirms the extent to which Amir has never really fitted in. The attainment of Farid's respect coincides with Amir finally feeling more comfortable in his home country.

The tensions between the Pashtun and Hazara ethnic groups also form a thread throughout the novel. The teasing and bullying of Ali and Hassan occur because of their ethnicity, and the befriending by Baba and Amir of these Hazaras puts them on the wrong side of the ethnic divide. As such Baba would seem to be more advanced in his opinions than many of his fellow Afghans, and passes this liberal attitude onto his son. However, Amir is not confident enough to act on these beliefs until the end of the novel. When he tells his father-in-law to refer to Sohrab by name rather than by his ethnic group he shows that he now has this confidence. It is significant that Farid,

> **CONTEXT**
>
> Pashtun and Hazara are just two of the ethnic groups which make up Afghanistan's diverse racial mix. Other groups include Tajiks, Uzbeks and nomadic Aimak.

a confirmed Afghan, demonstrates the same discriminatory views as were present in Amir's childhood, showing that this is still a problem in contemporary Afghanistan. The suggestion that Hosseini seems to be making is that it is the lack of respect for different peoples which underlies all the problems in Afghanistan.

Hassan, Ali and Sohrab, as Hazaras, are shown as being much more spiritual and devout than Amir and his father. Amir refers to Hassan having 'prayed the morning *namaz* with Ali' (p. 23) while he is still emerging from his bed, having taken no part in the morning prayers. However, this devotion is not sufficient for the Taliban to spare them because they follow the Shi'a branch of Islam, rather than the Sunni branch which the Taliban follow. As Hazaras and also Shi'a muslims, Hassan and his family struggle against both religious and ethnic persecution.

STORYTELLING

 CHECK THE BOOK
Storytelling is a key theme in Persian literature as exemplified by the classic text *One Thousand and One Nights* (sometimes called *The Arabian Nights*) in which Scheherazade keeps herself alive by telling her husband a new story every night. Her tales include famous stories such as 'Aladdin and His Magic Lamp', 'Ali Baba and the Forty Thieves' and 'The Seven Voyages of Sinbad'.

Storytelling is another theme which runs through the novel. The whole **narrative** is told to us as a story, with Amir setting the scene for us at the beginning and providing background, narrating the story from its end point. As a **narrator** he constantly intrudes into the story, **foreshadowing** events to come, and reminding us that we are being told a story.

The **symbolism** of this idea is reinforced when Amir tells us of the stories he would read to Hassan as a child and then his development into a professional storyteller, a novelist. As such, the artificial nature of what we are told is regularly foregrounded. The constant reminder that we are being told a story forces the reader to interpret it for its underlying meanings, rather than simply accept the narrative at face value.

In addition, when Amir informs Wahid that he is a writer, Wahid tells him to write about Afghanistan, but Amir says he is not that sort of writer. It is clear that Hosseini, who is from a background similar in many ways to Amir, is writing about Afghanistan, so begs the question why Amir does not. This concept is associated with Amir's difficulty in accepting his Afghan heritage, but also places Amir as a fiction writer, i.e. someone who makes things up, rather than describing the real world. As such, the story he is narrating to us demonstrates a change brought about by his visit back to Afghanistan. *The Kite Runner* therefore represents a story which Amir has found too hard to relate before, both in terms of the harsh reality of his homeland and also the internal landscape which he has previously found it too painful to explore.

The stories which are told in the novel all have symbolic value because they are stories of friendship and loyalty. The stories which Amir reads to Hassan form a large part of their bond, but also provide Amir with another way to tease and bully Hassan. However, it is these stories which lead to Hassan naming his son, a reference back to the connection between Amir and Hassan and a gesture of forgiveness from Hassan for Amir's behaviour.

The ultimate reconciliation of Amir and his father, just prior to his death, comes at the moment when Amir discovers Soraya reading his stories to Baba. It is through this act of acceptance that Amir finally realises his father's love for him.

Other stories in the novel come in the form of the letters from Hassan and Rahim Khan and Rahim Khan's tale of his time in Kabul after Amir and his father left. These give us an alternative perspective from Amir's and allow us a little distance with which to judge how truthful Amir's narrative has been.

The stories in the novel are constantly bound up with teaching and learning, whether it is Amir's mother's book being the source of her teaching materials, Amir failing to teach Hassan to read, or Soraya teaching her servant to read. So, when Amir has finally learned his lesson he buys a copy of the book which he used to share with Hassan, misleading and teasing him. He now plans to use it to build a bridge to Sohrab, returning to the beginning now that he understands what he should have known all along.

THE INTERACTION OF PERSONAL AND GLOBAL HISTORY

While *The Kite Runner* is the story of Amir, Hassan and their father, it is also a story about the events in Afghanistan from the

---

CONTEXT

The term for a piece of fiction which addresses the act of storytelling as one of its themes is 'metafiction'. It literally means 'fiction about fiction'. By featuring a novelist as the **protagonist**, relating the story to us as a potentially fictionalised account of the real story, *The Kite Runner* could be viewed as a metafiction.

 CHECK THE POEM

Amir cannot bring himself to confront Afghanistan's problems in his writing. This predicament is similar to that expressed in Hayden Carruth's poem 'On Being Asked to Write a Poem Against the War in Vietnam' (1992), which examines the futility of being a poet when faced with the topic of war.

CHECK THE BOOK

The interweaving of fact and fiction is also a feature of the books in Pat Barker's *Regeneration* trilogy: *Regeneration*, *The Eye in the Door* and *The Ghost Road* (1991–5). These address the events of the First World War and include in their character list the real-life war poet, Siegfried Sassoon.

1970s to the first years of the twenty-first century. Hosseini uses the story of Amir to tell the story of Afghanistan at the same time, intertwining the two so that the history does not become either a backdrop or an interruption, but an integral part of the plot and narrative.

There are many examples of this, starting with the sounds of the coup in 1973 intruding on Amir's childhood as the first real signs of what is to come. Other examples include the flight of Amir and Baba from Khabul, Baba's confrontation with the Russian soldier, the Taliban killing Hassan, and Assef becoming a leader in the Taliban. Perhaps the greatest **symbolic** interaction of the story and historical events is the banning by the Taliban of kite flying and fighting. By making this sport the centre of the novel, Hosseini is able to show to what extent the Taliban were opposed to the desires and wishes of ordinary Afghan people. For more on the real events that underlie the story, and are bound up in it, see **Background: Historical background**.

LANGUAGE AND STYLE

The style of language which an author chooses for a particular character is created by a combination of the structure of their sentences, their choice of vocabulary and the **imagery** they use. These things can tell you a great deal about a character – their level of education, their personality type (e.g. enthusiastic, timid, etc.) – and can also change to show changes in the character.

Almost the whole of *The Kite Runner*, with one or two exceptions, is narrated by Amir. He tells it from the viewpoint of an adult looking back across his life. As it is a personal narration it is quite an informal, conversational style, similar to dialogue, rather than a self-consciously literary style of writing.

Amir's narrative voice is fairly consistent across most of the novel. However, there is a development in vocabulary and sentence structure as he moves from talking about his childhood years to talking about his adult life.

When relating his childhood, especially in the chapters leading up to the attack on Hassan, he tends to use childlike language, for example, 'he never told on me' (p. 4); or a childlike simplicity of description, 'They clapped for a long time. Afterward, people shook his hand' (p. 13). This style is already starting to show signs of maturity as the narrative reaches the point of Hassan's rape: the trauma of this moment is accompanied by a dropping away of the childlike tone.

Turning away from the alley, Amir says 'I was weeping' (p. 67). He does not use the more familiar word 'crying' which we might have expected. Then, having decided that he was a coward because he ran away, he tells us that he 'actually aspired to cowardice' (p. 68). This is an adult notion and an adult way of expressing it. At the end of that chapter, as he is held and hugged by Baba, the tone of voice reflects the security he feels in that moment by reverting to a simple childish voice, but this, like the feeling of security that Amir feels, does not last and by the start of the next chapter we are back to a more sophisticated prose with complex **compound sentences**. This is the style which remains for most of the rest of the novel.

Other changes occur to Amir's voice during times of stress or extreme anxiety, such as during the rape, in his fight with Assef and while recovering afterwards. At these points the sentence structure changes and becomes hesitant and broken to reflect the fragmentation of Amir's mind. Following Sohrab's suicide attempt, the narration enters the present tense, resulting in a more urgent and immediate voice: 'They won't let me in. I see them wheel him through a set of double doors and I follow' (p. 300).

Rahim Khan's voice is a little more graceful and less straightforward than Amir's, reflecting his greater age and different temperament. For instance, when talking about Kabul after Amir and Baba left he says, 'No one to greet, no one to sit down with for *chai*, no one to share stories with, just *Roussi* soldiers patrolling the streets' (p. 178). This repetitive structure, more like poetry than prose, is typical of how Rahim Khan speaks, both in his direct speech and in his letter.

> **CONTEXT**
>
> A 'writer's voice' is the term used to describe the individual writing style of a particular author. It can be defined at the smallest level in terms of word choice, grammar, punctuation, but also at the larger level of theme, the character's journey and use of dialogue.

**CHECK
THE BOOK**

The technique of
using letters and a
range of **first-
person narrators**
has been used to
construct whole
novels. One famous
example is Bram
Stoker's *Dracula*
(1897).

In contrast, Hassan's voice is written in a style which seems to have a more foreign cadence than either Rahim Khan's or Amir's. Of course, Amir's later voice is reflective of a character who has spent many years in the USA, and Rahim Khan's is of an intellectual man who has studied literature. Hassan has learned to read later in life and most of his writing and reading, we can assume, would be associated with his religion. So, the rhythm of his language reflects the lack of a Western influence, a more studied and less fluent style, and his greater familiarity with the rhythms of religious writing. Sentences such as 'I am hopeful that one day I will hold one of your letters in my hands and read of your life in America. Perhaps a photograph of you will even grace our eyes' (p. 189) exemplify both these aspects.

QUESTION

Examine Hassan's patterns of speech as reported by Amir and the voice we are presented with in his letter. How do they differ? Does the introduction of the voice in the letter change our perceptions of Hassan?

Hassan is also responsible for one of the key **motifs** of the novel, the phrase 'For you a thousand times over' (p. 59). This is representative of the slightly more formal style which we see in his letter, but also gives a good representation of unquestioned loyalty. Thus, when Amir uses this phrase to Sohrab at the end of the novel, we understand the transformation that has taken place in him, and his acceptance of the power and grace of an older, more spiritual form of language.

NARRATIVE TECHNIQUE AND STRUCTURE

The Kite Runner is written as a single story told to us by the **narrator**, Amir. He is telling it from a point in time at the end of the story, with knowledge of how everything turns out. As a result, all of his recollections are coloured by knowledge of what is to come. This results in a number of **narrative** techniques being used.

One of these can be seen in the fact that a level of adult understanding and rationalising overlays all of the childhood events which we are told about in the first third of the novel. Thus when we are told the stories from Amir's childhood there are two perspectives at work, the child's perception of events, and the reworked and possibly misremembered memories of the adult. As with anyone looking back on events from a distance in time, we must be aware that the details of the far past may have been changed or granted undue importance in the person's mind. This is especially true of a man like Amir who carries a great deal of guilt over events in his past. As a result it is crucial to notice the number of stories which Amir tells us which paint him in a poor light. He is attempting to portray himself as the 'bad guy' because his guilt tells him he deserves it. This technique is often referred to as 'unreliable narration' whereby we cannot necessarily trust the story we are told by an **unreliable narrator,** or the interpretation that they put on events, and as readers we must work to 'read between the lines' and make up our own minds.

The story is told from its chronological end point, so that Amir frequently **foreshadows** events which are yet to come. Using this technique a storyteller undercuts current events by revealing they will not last, as at the end of Chapter 5, 'that was the winter that Hassan stopped smiling' (p. 41). The technique is also used to build tension by revealing a small piece of information about events to come, making the reader want to read on and find out what happens next, as at the end of Chapters 1 and 2, and in particular at the end of Chapter 4, 'I never got to finish that sentence. / Because suddenly Afghanistan changed forever' (p. 30).

This technique continues to be used after the revelation of Hassan's rape, but not as frequently as before, and not usually as a chapter ending. Instead, memories of earlier times are inserted into later chapters, so that the moment of the rape forms the central moment which earlier chapters look forward to and later chapters look back at.

It is at the moment of Hassan's rape that both the structure and style of the writing change. In terms of the structure, apart from the fragment of Chapter 1, the chapters leading up to the revelation of the attack in the alley are all told in a straightforward manner, although much of what we are told fills in details from the characters' lives prior to the kite fight. Stories unfold in a chronological manner leading up to the event. However, at the moment of the attack the narrative structure fractures and never fully resumes the linear structure of earlier chapters. As Amir witnesses the rape the narrative veers to other stories at other times, representing the desire of Amir's mind to avoid dealing with what he is seeing.

CONTEXT

Although not formally split, *The Kite Runner* exists in three sections: Afghanistan, the USA, Afghanistan and Pakistan. This is a common structure for storytelling: see, for example, E. M. Forster's *A Passage to India* (1924) and Ian McEwan's *Atonement* (2001). A similar three-act structure is often used in film-making: 'set-up', 'confrontation' and 'resolution'.

 CHECK THE FILM

The Sixth Sense, starring Bruce Willis (1999), relies on the technique of foreshadowing as a major part of its plot structure.

This is also the point at which the style of storytelling changes. Up until this point the stories have largely been related to us as things that happened. They have mostly been 'told' to us, unembellished, in much the way a child relates a story, with the interpretation and emotion of the events explained to us. At the point of fracture, the adult voice of Amir takes over and events from then on are largely 'shown' events. These are sometimes presented out of order, or with gaps between them, and it is up to us as readers to provide our own interpretations from the events described and their **juxtaposition**.

The Kite Runner could be seen as an example of the type of story known as a fable. This is a story, often featuring animals or inanimate objects rather than humans, but which is meant to convey a moral lesson. *The Kite Runner* does this by constantly reinforcing what is good and what is bad through Amir's guilt and his need to atone.

Another way to describe the story would be as an **allegory**. This is a type of story where a small **narrative** stands for a larger one (e.g. *The Lion, the Witch and the Wardrobe* as an allegory for Christianity). In the case of *The Kite Runner*, Amir's journey of redemption becomes an accompaniment to a description of the trials of the Afghan people; his search for reconciliation can be seen as representative of their search for peace and self-determination.

As well as the main plot, involving Amir, Baba, Hassan and Sohrab, there are a number of sub-plots including the stories of the mothers of Amir and Hassan, Rahim Khan and Assef. The most prominent of these is the story of Soraya, Amir's wife. Her story is provided as a complement to Amir's. She, like him, carries a burden of guilt and shame from events in her past. Her role is to show how it is possible to recover from such a shame, and so provide hope for Amir.

Another technique employed to lend depth to the narrative is the inclusion of various dreams. The reporting of dreams is a common technique used in literature. An author may use it to **foreshadow** events to come, with seemingly prophetic dreams; to add a level of **symbolism**; or to provide hidden knowledge that characters are unable to see for themselves. Hosseini uses dreams in the text for all three purposes. Hassan's dream on the day of the kite-fighting tournament seems to be prophetic of the danger which is waiting

CHECK THE BOOK
The most famous fables are *Aesop's Fables*, in which moral lessons are told via animals. Aesop was a slave who lived in Greece in the sixth century BC. Some of his fables have become standard folk tales, e.g. 'The Ant and the Grasshopper', 'The Tortoise and the Hare' and 'The Boy Who Cried Wolf'.

CHECK THE BOOK
C. S. Lewis's *The Lion, the Witch and the Wardrobe* (1950) is both a fable – in that it uses animal characters to tell a story with a moral message – and an allegory – with Aslan representing Christ who dies and is resurrected as the saviour of Narnia.

for him in the seemingly safe day before him; the dream which Amir remembers during the attack on Hassan is symbolic of his feelings of being lost, but also his guilt at being safe; and Amir's later dream, when recovering from Assef's attack, of wrestling the black bear himself, provides the revelation – both to him and to us – that he has finally reconciled himself with his father.

CHECK THE POEM

The use of dreams both as literary device and as a subject is common in literature. In his poem, 'A Dream Within a Dream' (1849), Edgar Allan Poe considers the possibility that life itself is simply a dream.

PART FOUR

CRITICAL PERSPECTIVES

READING CRITICALLY

This section provides a range of critical perspectives on *The Kite Runner* and gives a broad overview of key debates, interpretations and theories proposed since the novel was published. This text has produced a variety of interpretations and responses, many of them shaped by the critics' own backgrounds and historical contexts.

No single view of the text should be seen as dominant. You must arrive at your own judgements by questioning the perspectives described, and by developing your own critical insights. Objective analysis is a skill achieved through coupling close reading with an informed understanding of the key ideas, related texts and background information relevant to the text. These elements are all crucial in enabling you to assess the interpretations of other readers, and even to view works of criticism as texts in themselves. The ability to read critically will serve you well both in your study of *The Kite Runner*, and in any critical writing, presentation or further work you undertake.

CRITICAL HISTORY

The Kite Runner (2003) has not yet gained a body of extended literary criticism. However, upon its publication and in the years since, it has been the subject of a number of reviews and profiles and Khaled Hosseini has given interviews about the novel. These form a useful guide to the text and its reception to date.

Initial reviews of a novel try to give the reading public a sense of the storyline of the novel and some indications of whether or not they might like to buy it. This is very different from the intentions of critical writing, which assume that the reader is familiar with the text and wants to explore it more deeply. However, this does not necessarily mean that reviews are superficial, but simply that they

CHECK THE BOOK

Malcolm Bradbury gives excellent overviews of recent critical movements in literature in his companion books, *The Modern British Novel* (rev. edn 2001) and *The Modern American Novel* (rev. edn 1992).

try to deal with the book as a whole, rather than concentrating on individual aspects of it.

The immediate reception of *The Kite Runner*, upon its publication in 2003, was positive, with Edward Hower in the *New York Times* commenting on the 'powerful' nature of the novel, praising it for its ability to mix the personal with the political and the historical: 'Khaled Hosseini gives us a vivid and engaging story that reminds us how long his people have been struggling to triumph over the forces of violence – forces that continue to threaten them even today' (*New York Times*, 3 August 2003).

Many other reviewers also picked up on this aspect of the novel, including Amelia Hill ('An Afghan hounded by his past', *Observer*, 7 September 2003) and Sue Bond ('*The Kite Runner* by Khaled Hosseini', *Asian Review of Books*, 19 July 2003).

However, both Hill and Bond wrote that they thought *The Kite Runner* appeared to be the first novel written by an Afghan in English and aimed at Western readers. This is an opinion which has become accepted as fact. It does, however, ignore *Afghanistan, Where God Only Comes to Weep* by Siba Shakib, published a year earlier. What is certain, however, is that *The Kite Runner* was the first novel of its type to achieve such prominence and to impact so greatly on Western readers.

According to the author's own website, since its publication the novel has spent over two years on the *New York Times* bestseller list, has been translated into forty-two languages and published in forty-eight countries. Certainly, this widespread readership offers some idea of the popularity of the text. Additionally, in 2006, it was awarded the Penguin/Orange Reading Group (UK) Book of the Year prize.

The novel has not been free of criticism. David Kipen, reviewing it for Hosseini's local newspaper the *San Francisco Chronicle* on 8 June 2003, pointed out the heavy-handed use of themes in the novel and questioned whether it would have been such a success without the US war in Afghanistan. Both of these seem to be reasonable points which other reviewers appear to have overlooked in their speed to praise a novel hailed as the first of its kind.

 CHECK THE NET

ReviewsOfBooks.com is a useful site which gathers together links to online reviews. For reviews of *The Kite Runner*, go to **www.reviews ofbooks.com** and type 'Kite Runner' into the search box.

CONTEXT

The popularity of certain books is increasingly being generated by recommendations from television 'book clubs' such as those run by *Richard & Judy* in the UK and *Oprah* in the USA. Recommended titles include Julia Gregson's *East of the Sun* (2008) and Chimamanda Ngozi Adichie's *Half of a Yellow Sun* (2006).

CHECK THE NET

Matthew Thomas Miller's article 'The Kite Runner critiqued: New Orientalism goes to the big screen' was published online on 5 January 2008 at CommonDreams.org. Go to **www.common dreams.org** and click on 'Archives', then 'Views 2008', where the article is listed under January.

However, a sharper critique of the novel comes in Matthew Thomas Miller's article, '*The Kite Runner* critiqued: New Orientalism goes to the big screen'. Miller criticises the novel for promoting the concept of 'new orientalism' (discussed further in the section on post-colonialism below) whereby the ruling regimes of the countries of the Middle East are portrayed as cruel and repressive as opposed to the free, liberal and safe nature of the West and, in particular, the USA. While this argument can perhaps be made based upon aspects of *The Kite Runner*, it does neglect Hosseini's attempts to portray the ordinary people of Afghanistan as friendly, intelligent and welcoming, and show the people as the victims of the extremists who are in charge, rather than characterising the whole race in the same way.

CONTEMPORARY APPROACHES

There is no evidence that Hosseini set out to write a novel with any particular basis in the various movements of literary or critical theory. However, purely as a production of Hosseni's own reading and the point in history at which *The Kite Runner* was written, it is possible to see how a number of different theories can be applied to the text to create greater understanding.

The main literary movements in the twentieth century were **modernism** and what can be seen as both its successor and its continuation, **postmodernism**. From the time of its writing, and its setting, *The Kite Runner* falls most clearly in the latter movement, but it is also clearly a part of the movement known as post-colonialism, which encompasses those texts produced either in formerly colonised countries – such as India or Pakistan – or those produced by the emigrants from such countries. In addition, it would be possible to examine *The Kite Runner* from a Marxist perspective, looking at the roles of class and economic power in the novel, or by using the principles of psychoanalysis to examine the way **symbols** and dreams work in the text.

MODERNISM/POSTMODERNISM

The movement known as modernism started in France in the mid nineteenth century, but became more widespread at the beginning of the twentieth century and especially after the First World War. As a literary movement it was a reaction against **realist narratives** which had previously dominated. These were often epic novels covering long periods of time with an **omniscient narrator** providing their view of events in a linear fashion, for example Jane Austen's *Pride and Prejudice* (1813) and George Eliot's *Middlemarch* (1871–2). Modernism embraced experiment to closely examine personal experience, for example Virginia Woolf's 'The Mark on the Wall' (1917) was written as a **stream of consciousness**. Narratives covered much shorter periods of time – James Joyce's *Ulysses* (1922), which takes place on a single day – and concentrated on the internal life of the characters via **first-person narrators**.

While it overturned the structures of realism, modernism created structures of its own. Postmodernism, as an outgrowth of modernism, maintains many of the features of its predecessor, but also aims to deconstruct such formal arrangements: fragmentation and fracture are used to create meaning from the **juxtaposition** of individual sections of text and the contrast between them.

The Kite Runner does not fit easily into the strict mould of a postmodern novel with much of the narrative being of a realist style which could be compared to the works of Dickens or Austen. However, some of the features of postmodernism do appear in the narrative. Amir is clearly burdened by his past and, as such, we distrust what he tells us and are forced to interpret his words in order to find an 'objective' truth. The use of an **unreliable narrator** is a common feature of postmodern texts: it both undermines the power of the narrator's voice as the source of all information and also foregrounds the notion of all experience as personal and individual.

In addition, the text is not continuous and, at key moments, fractures to present us with a mosaic of impressions and experiences which do not advance the narrative but give extra depth and colour

CHECK THE POEM

The modernist movement in literature was not solely tied to prose, but was widely explored in poetry as well. The foremost example of this is T. S. Eliot's *The Waste Land* (1922).

CHECK THE BOOK

A **postmodern** text which takes the idea of **narrative** fracture to its logical extreme is Italo Calvino's *If on a Winter's Night a Traveller* (1979), which features ten consecutive opening chapters to ten separate novels.

to both those moments of the story and our impression of the **narrator**. The most prominent example of this is during Hassan's rape when Amir's mind suddenly conjures memories and remembered dreams to divert him from what is happening. However, each of these diversions provides insight into the workings of Amir's mind and the reasoning behind his feelings about Hassan.

POST-COLONIALISM

Although a **postmodern** novel in certain aspects, *The Kite Runner* can be more easily situated within the tradition of **post-colonial** fiction as formulated most famously in Edward Said's 1978 book, *Orientalism*. This movement deals with the fiction emerging from countries which were once colonised by others. Said attempted to address the ways in which the West viewed the peoples of Eastern countries as lesser, or sub-human in order to justify their colonisation; such views were reflected in literature and other cultural forms. Post-colonialism examines the way the cultural identity of such a country has been affected by colonisation, and it looks at the attempts to reclaim the cultural heritage made after independence has been gained. It also looks at the texts produced by those people who have left to live in the colonising countries. The ethnic groups formed in these countries are known as the diaspora.

The Kite Runner is a crucial text in this regard because it is the one of the first texts written in English by an Afghan dealing with Afghanistan and the many changes of rule and various types of subjugation which its people have suffered. In some ways, given the earlier colonial occupation of Afghanistan by the British, *The Kite Runner* is a typical post-colonial novel in that it uses the language of a former oppressor to tell the story and reclaim a sense of Afghan identity. However, the subsequent periods of independence, Russian occupation and civil war make this analysis more problematic. So far there is little work on this aspect of the novel, but it would seem to be a rich seam for future exploration.

CHECK THE BOOK

Anne Tyler's *Digging to America* (2006) is set in the USA. It describes the mixing of American, Iranian and Korean cultures and also addresses the topic of adoption.

As a diasporic novel written by and about an Afghanistan emigrant, part of *The Kite Runner* examines what it means to be an Afghan in the USA, living as part of an Afghan community which is situated away from the home country. A common feature of this kind of novel is that the community in diaspora becomes a more concentrated form of the society which it has left behind, holding more rigidly to its traditions and customs. *The Kite Runner* describes this phenomenon: the country left behind undergoes such strife and change that the Afghan–American community forms a repository of customs which may be changed or lost in the home county. Amir's return to Afghanistan in the novel allows for a contrast to be drawn between the community in exile and the society remaining in Afghanistan.

In recent years, especially following the attacks in the USA on 11 September 2001 and the subsequent wars in Afghanistan and Iraq, a 'new orientalism' has been identified by critics who believe that the peoples of those and surrounding countries are being classed once more as 'different' by the Western propaganda surrounding the conflicts. *The Kite Runner*, however, works against this trend by giving the people of Afghanistan a human face. This even extends to the Taliban character of Assef who, while we may not like him or identify with him, we can at least understand as being human and acting from human motives.

CHECK THE BOOK

The perceived return towards 'orientalism', especially post-9/11, is examined in depth in M. Shahid Alam's book *Challenging the New Orientalism: Dissenting Essays on the 'War Against Islam'* (2007).

MARXISM

Marxist critics examine literary texts in terms of the social and political influences on a work and how these are represented in the finished work. As such they interpret **narratives** in terms of the representation of the balance of power between different societal groups. In English literature, this often resolves itself as an examination of the wealth and power belonging to the upper classes as opposed to the lack of these things in the working classes. In a novel like *The Kite Runner*, this distinction is drawn on ethnic lines, between the Pashtuns and the Hazaras, as well as the class divides of master and servant.

The Kite Runner displays the disparity in wealth and power between Amir and his family, and Hassan and his servants. This reaches its ultimate expression in the 'ethnic cleansing' of the Hazara people during the massacre of Mazir-i-Shairif.

Allied with this is another focus of Marxism, namely the way in which religion is used to control the masses. Amir's people, the Pashtuns, are shown with less of a respect for religion than the Hazaras. Baba is dismissive, Amir is largely indifferent, and someone like Assef uses his religion as it suits him to further his own ends. Hassan and Sohrab are shown as much more obedient and mindful of their faith and so, according to Marxist theory, exist under a greater degree of subjugation.

Along with the descriptions of life in Afghanistan, the novel and its circumstances of writing, also allow for a reading which compares the West – in particular the USA – with life in Afghanistan. As such a Marxist critic could examine the way in which capitalism is represented in both Amir's **narration** and in Hosseini's writing as a whole.

PSYCHOANALYSIS

A psychoanalytic approach to literary criticism involves using ideas from Sigmund Freud's theories of psychoanalysis. Just as Freudian analysis attempts to identify **symbolism** and concealed meanings in the thoughts and dreams of patients, so the same approach can be taken to literary texts, treating them as the 'dreams' of the writer. As such, it is possible to read texts in ways which reveal more about both the characters and the writer.

In *The Kite Runner*, a number of aspects become apparent, including the lack of any prominent female figures in the novel. With his mother dead, Amir's journey can be seen in terms of attempting to please his absent mother. As such, he is also seeking a mother figure, which he fails to find in Baba, but finds to some extent in the compassionate and understanding side of Rahim Khan's character. A repeated symbol is the **motif** of kite flying.

This is a child's pursuit, but one with still immense importance for Amir, suggesting a stunted emotional growth which has never moved beyond childhood.

This kind of analysis could be applied to many aspects in *The Kite Runner*, using a schema such as Freud's *The Interpretation of Dreams* (1899). In this book, Freud provides examples of dreams and his method for interpreting them as a way of unpacking the symbolic nature of dream images for understanding the deeper workings of the psyche. The influence of this text can be seen in the way dreams are used in *The Kite Runner* at key moments. Whether it is Hassan's dream of success but also lurking danger, on the night before the kite tournament (Chapter 7); Amir's remembered dream of being lost in a snowstorm and then rescued, recounted at the moment of Hassan's attack (Chapter 7); or Amir's dream of himself wrestling his father's black bear (Chapter 23), when recovering in hospital from Assef's beating – all of these dreams are used to symbolise parts of the mind of the dreamer and also the themes of the novel as a whole.

 QUESTION

Psychoanalytic theory suggests analysing books as though they were dreams. In what ways can the story of *The Kite Runner* be seen as Amir's dream?

PART FIVE

BACKGROUND

KHALED HOSSEINI'S LIFE AND WORKS

QUESTION
Khaled Hosseini was working as a doctor when he wrote *The Kite Runner*. How would the story be different if Amir had been a doctor rather than a writer?

Khaled Hosseini was born in Kabul, Afghanistan, on 4 March 1965. His father was a diplomat in the Foreign Ministry of the Afghan government and his mother was a high-school teacher, teaching history and the Persian language, Farsi. The family lived in Afghanistan and Iran until 1976 when his father took a post in Paris. Plans for the family to return to Afghanistan in 1980 were abandoned following the communist overthrow of the government and the invasion by the Soviet Army. Instead the family was granted political asylum in the USA and in September 1980 moved to San Jose, California.

Hosseini graduated from Independence High School in San Jose in 1984 and went on to study biology at Santa Clara University, a Jesuit-affiliated university based just a few kilometres from San Jose. Graduating from here in 1988 he enrolled in the School of Medicine at the San Diego campus of the University of California. He was granted his licence to practise as a doctor in 1993. He completed the final stage of his medical training as a resident at Cedars-Sinai Hospital in Los Angeles until 1996. He then went on to be a practising doctor until 2004, specialising in internal medicine.

CONTEXT
The United Nations High Commission for Refugees (UNHCR) dedicates itself to the protection of refugees around the world, helping them to return safely to their homelands, or to resettle in other countries.

In 2001, while still a practising doctor, Hosseini started writing the novel which would become *The Kite Runner*. It was published in 2003 by Bloomsbury Publishing Plc. He has since written a second novel, *A Thousand Splendid Suns*, published by Riverhead Books in May 2007. Where *The Kite Runner* is mostly the story of Afghan men, this second novel focuses on the lives of women in Afghanistan before and during the rule of the Taliban.

In 2006, Hosseini became a Goodwill Envoy for the United Nations High Commission for Refugees (UNHCR). He has used his success to aid various projects contributing to the rebuilding of Afghanistan. He now lives in northern California with his wife and their two children.

A film of *The Kite Runner* was released in 2007 to a mixed reception. It has been nominated for thirteen different awards of varying prominence and has won three of them. It was nominated for the Golden Globe Award for both Best Foreign Language Film and Best Original Score – Motion Picture, and the Academy Award for Best Original Score but failed to win these. The film was banned in Afghanistan because of the rape scene and the depiction of ethnic tensions.

HISTORICAL BACKGROUND

THE RULE OF KINGS IN AFGHANISTAN, TO 1973

Throughout the nineteenth century, Afghanistan was largely under the influence of the United Kingdom as part of its occupation of the Indian subcontinent. This was an aspect of what was called the 'Great Game' whereby the Russian and British empires contended for control of the region. This control was maintained by a series of three Anglo-Afghan Wars, which occurred in 1838–42, 1878–80 and in 1919.

Afghanistan finally achieved a measure of independence in 1919 after King Amanullah Khan (whose wife, like Amir's in *The Kite Runner*, was named Soraya) took power and began the move for self-government which started the Third Anglo-Afghan War. Full independence was granted in 1921.

Amanullah Khan's reforms were considered by some as too radical, and he was forced to abdicate in January 1929 by forces led by Habibullah Kalakani, who assumed power. Mohammed Nadir Khan – a cousin of Amanullah – then defeated and killed Habibullah Kalakani just nine months later. This is the man after whom Amir's home district of Kabul was named: Wazir Nadir Khan.

Nadir Khan was assassinated in 1933, and was succeeded by Mohammad Zahir Shah, Nadir Khan's nineteen-year-old son. There followed an extended period of peace in Afghanistan which lasted until former Prime Minister Mohammad Sardar Daoud Khan, the king's cousin and brother-in-law, seized power in a military coup on 17 July 1973.

> **CONTEXT**
>
> The more recent competition in the same area between the USA and the USSR has been known as the 'New Great Game'.

THE REPUBLIC, UNREST AND CIVIL WAR IN AFGHANISTAN, 1973–92

CHECK THE BOOK

M. E. Hirsh's *Kabul* (1986) is a family's story which starts on the day of the coup and ends with the Soviet invasion in 1979.

Afghanistan lasted as a republic under Daoud Khan for just five years. On 27 April 1978 the People's Democratic Party of Afghanistan (PDPA) overthrew Daoud Khan's administration, and he and his family were killed.

In 1979, following a series of uprisings and heavy reprisals, the government of the new Democratic Republic was forced to call on Russian troops to help quell the disturbances. The Soviet Army carried out military missions against US-supported Islamic rebels for the next nine years, finally withdrawing its troops in February 1989. However, the Soviet Union continued to lend aid to the Afghan government until its collapse at the beginning of the 1990s.

THE ISLAMIC STATE OF AFGHANISTAN, 1992–2004

Without the support of the Soviet Union, the PDPA government was vulnerable and was overthrown on 18 April 1992 by a coalition of resistance fighters. The Democratic Republic was replaced by the Islamic State of Afghanistan. However, following the withdrawal of the common enemy – the Soviet Union – the different groups in Afghanistan turned on each other, creating a civil war between the various classes, ethnic groups, militias, etc.

CHECK THE BOOK

A range of different war poetry, including poems by writers such as Seamus Heaney, Ted Hughes and W. B. Yeats, can be found in *101 Poems Against War* (2003) edited by Paul Keegan and Matthew Hollis.

As a reaction against this fighting, and due to a lack of Pashtun representation in the government, the Taliban, a group of highly religious scholars and fighters, emerged from the southern province of Kandahar. By the end of 2000 the Taliban had control of the majority of the country. The only opposition to them at the time of the attacks on 11 September 2001 was the Afghan Northern Alliance, a small group in the north-east, which continued to be recognised by the United Nations as the legitimate government of Afghanistan.

Following the events of 11 September 2001, the USA and a coalition of allies attacked Afghanistan in an effort to overthrow the government. This was because of the Taliban's refusal to help the

USA to find Al Qaeda terrorist forces hiding in Afghanistan and, in particular, to help the search for Osama bin Laden, the man believed to be in charge of Al Qaeda. After the removal of the Taliban government, an interim authority was formed; Hamid Karzai led this authority for six months. At the end of this time Karzai was appointed president by a group led by the former king, Zahir Shah. On 9 October 2004, Afghanistan's first democratic election was held: Karzai was officially voted into the presidency.

At the time of writing, elements of the Taliban and other extremist Islamic groups are still fighting in Afghanistan against the coalition's troops. It would seem that the story of Afghanistan's turmoil is not yet at an end.

LITERARY BACKGROUND

The Kite Runner has been described in reviews as representing a new kind of novel, one in which the story of life in Afghanistan has been written by an Afghan but in English, rather than appearing in translation. However, in other ways, *The Kite Runner* is embedded firmly in the history of fiction in the English language. The influence of other texts is reflected in both the plot and the construction of *The Kite Runner* and, whether conscious or unconscious, these **allusions** make the reading of the novel all the richer.

In many ways, *The Kite Runner* is a traditional **realist** novel in which a story is told by a **narrator** with a strong plot which leads the reader through, telling the life of the main character. In this way, the novel is part of a tradition going back to the publication of *Pamela* by Samuel Richardson in 1740, a book often credited as being the first 'real' novel. This book was the story of a maid and her master told through a series of letters, in the form known as **epistolary**. This is a style borrowed by Hosseini for *The Kite Runner* whereby other characters' voices, and some key plot information, are presented to us in letter form.

 CHECK THE BOOK

Love and War in Afghanistan (2004) is a set of stories from the people of northern Afghanistan collected by Alexander Klaits and Gulchin Gulmamadova-Klaits. It provides personal perspectives of life in Afghanistan during the years of war and oppression.

CHECK THE BOOK

Ian Watt's *The Rise of the Novel: Studies in Defoe, Richardson and Fielding* (rev. edn 2001) provides an excellent overview of the origins of the novel and its rise to become a dominant literary form.

QUESTION

The Kite Runner deals with very recent history. In what ways might this be both a help and a hindrance to an understanding of the book?

Charles Dickens's *Great Expectations* (1860–1) would seem to have influenced *The Kite Runner* heavily. As with Hosseini's novel, this is the story of a character's life as narrated by him. However, it is also a story in which an event in the childhood of the **narrator** has effects for the rest of his life, both internally and externally. In a similar vein is Victor Hugo's *Les Misérables* (1862), which Hosseini actually references in Chapter 24. This too is a novel about a man with events in his past for which he is seeking atonement. It is also a novel in which the historical setting plays a large part.

In dealing with the conflicts in Afghanistan, Hosseini aligns himself with other writers who try to make sense of war. These include the famous works of the 'war poets' such as Wilfred Owen or Siegfried Sassoon, and novels such as Sebastian Faulks's *Birdsong* (1993), Michael Frayn's *Spies* (2002) and Pat Barker's *The Ghost Road* (1995). In this respect, and in the setting of much of the novel, *The Kite Runner* can also be seen as an **historical novel**, i.e. one which is set in a period prior to the time of writing. Although the events of the last third of the novel are contemporary to the time of writing, the whole story rests on its historical roots.

The most prominent literary antecedents of *The Kite Runner* come in the form of those novels which are considered to be part of the movement known as **post-colonialism**. There are many novels in this category including Arundhati Roy's *The God of Small Things*, which won the Booker Prize for literature in 1997.

In Amir's case – and for Hosseini himself – having been a child at the time of his emigration from Afghanistan, they are in fact similar to the second-generation post-colonial writers who consider their 'homeland' from a greater distance and with a more romantic view. Prominent examples of similar post-colonial fiction include Zadie Smith's *White Teeth* (2000) and Monica Ali's *Brick Lane* (2003).

The Kite Runner's high profile has led to the release of a number of novels dealing with the same subject, and a higher profile in general for books dealing with Afghanistan and other countries which have previously been poorly understood in the West. These include Yasmina Khadra's *Swallows of Kabul* (2002), also set in Afghanistan; Jean Sasson's *Love in a Torn Land* (2007), set amongst the Kurdish people in Saddam Hussein's Iraq; Chimimanda Ngozi Adichie's *Purple Hibiscus* (2004), set in Nigeria; and Rajaa Alsanea's *Girls of Riyadh* (2005), set in Saudi Arabia.

QUESTION Since the events of 11 September 2001 and the publication of *The Kite Runner* in 2003, an array of books set in Afghanistan and other Middle Eastern countries has emerged. To what extent do you think these can be seen as belonging to a new category, separate from other post-colonial fiction?

World events	Khaled Hosseini's life	Literary events
		1740 Publication of *Pamela* by Samuel Richardson
		1813 *Pride and Prejudice* by Jane Austen
		1860–1 *Great Expectations* by Charles Dickens
		1871–2 *Middlemarch* by George Eliot
1914–18 First World War		**1917** 'Anthem for Doomed Youth' by Wilfred Owen
1919 Treaty of Versailles establishes the grounds of peace after the First World War and Afghanistan is granted a measure of independence		
1921 Afghanistan achieves full independence under King Amanullah Khan		
		1922 *Ulysses* by James Joyce
		1924 *A Passage to India* by E. M. Forster
		1927 *To the Lighthouse* by Virginia Woolf
1929 King Amanullah Khan is forced to abdicate by Habibullah Kalakani, who assumes power. He, in turn, is deposed nine months later by Mohammed Nadir Khan		
1933 Mohammed Nadir Khan is assassinated and is succeeded by his son Mohammad Zahir Shah		

World events	Khaled Hosseini's life	Literary events
1939 Outbreak of Second World War		
1945 End of Second World War; dropping of atomic bombs on Nagasaki and Hiroshima in Japan		
1945–91 Cold War		**1955** *Lolita* by Vladimir Nabokov
	1965 (4 March) Born in Kabul, Afghanistan	
	1970 Family moves to Tehran, Iran	
		1969 *The French Lieutenant's Woman* by John Fowles
1973 Prime Minister Mohammad Sardar Daoud Khan, the king's cousin and brother-in-law, seizes power in a military coup	**1973** Family moves back to Kabul	
	1976 Family moves to Paris	
1978 The People's Democratic Party of Afghanistan (PDPA) overthrows Daoud Khan's government		**1978** *Orientalism* by Edward Said
1979–89 Russian troops occupy Afghanistan lending aid to the government against the Mujahedin	**1980** Family seeks political asylum in the USA and settles in San Jose, California	
		1981 *Midnight's Children* by Salman Rushdie

World events	Khaled Hosseini's life	Literary events
	1984 Graduates from Independence High School in San Jose, California	
	1988 Gains a degree in biology from Santa Clara University, California	
	1989 Joins the University of California, San Diego, School of Medicine	**1989** *London Fields* by Martin Amis
1990–1 The Gulf War between UN coalition and Iraq following Iraq's invasion of Kuwait		
1992–2001 Under the new Islamic State of Afghanistan, the Taliban slowly take control of Afghanistan	**1993** Becomes a medical doctor and joins a residency programme in internal medicine at Cedars-Sinai Medical Center in Los Angeles	**1993** *Birdsong* by Sebastian Faulks
	1996 Completes his residency and becomes a practising doctor	**1997** *The God of Small Things* by Arundhati Roy
		2000 *White Teeth* by Zadie Smith
2001 onwards Following the attacks on the USA on 11 September 2001, a coalition of countries invades Afghanistan in an effort to find Al Qaeda operatives. They overthrow the rule of the Taliban who become a guerilla force attempting to oust the invaders	**2001** Starts writing *The Kite Runner*	

World events	Khaled Hosseini's life	Literary events
		2002 *Afghanistan, Where God Only Comes to Weep* by Siba Shakib
2003 USA and UK invade Iraq for the second time	2003 *The Kite Runner* is published	2003 *Brick Lane* by Monica Ali
2004 Hamid Karzai is voted president of Afghanistan		
	2006 Named a Goodwill Envoy for UNHCR	
	2007 Release of *The Kite Runner* (film); *A Thousand Splendid Suns* is published	

FURTHER READING

BOOKS BY KHALED HOSSEINI

The Kite Runner, 2003

A Thousand Splendid Suns, 2007

FILMS

The Kite Runner, 2007, directed by Marc Forster

CRITICISM

Links to articles and reviews of Khaled Hosseini's work, and an interview with the author, can be found online at **www.khaledhosseini.com**

WAR LITERATURE

Pat Barker, *The Ghost Road*, 1995

Sebastian Faulks, *Birdsong*, 1993

Michael Frayn, *Spies*, 2002

Paul Keegan and Matthew Hollis (eds), *101 Poems Against War*, 2003, including:

Hayden Carruth, 'On Being Asked to Write a Poem Against the War in Vietnam' (from a collection published 1992)

Seamus Heaney, 'Sophoclean', 2003

Ted Hughes, 'Six Young Men', 1957

Philip Larkin, 'MCMXIV', 1964

Wilfred Owen, 'Dulce et Decorum Est', 1917

W. B. Yeats, 'On Being Asked for a War Poem', 1919

POST-COLONIAL FICTION

Monica Ali, *Brick Lane*, 2003

Arundhati Roy, *The God of Small Things*, 1997

Zadie Smith, *White Teeth*, 2000

Anne Tyler, *Digging to America*, 2006

OTHER RELEVANT LITERATURE

Jane Austen, *Pride and Prejudice*, 1813

Charles Dickens, *Great Expectations*, 1860–1

Victor Hugo, *Les Misérables*, 1862

BACKGROUND READING

M. H. Abrams, *A Glossary of Literary Terms*, Harcourt Brace, 1981
   A useful reference work that covers most common literary terms and provides many articles
   outlining literary and critical movements

David Ayers, *Modernism: A Short Introduction*, Blackwell, 2004
   An introduction to the works of many prominent critics whose theories underpin the study of
 * modernism and postmodernism

Malcolm Bradbury, *The Modern American Novel*, Oxford University Press, 1992, and *The Modern British
Novel*, Penguin, 2001
   Two books which give an in-depth survey of literary movements and novels written in the English
   language from the start of the twentieth century

Joseph Campbell, *The Hero with a Thousand Faces* [1949], Fontana, 1993
   A book which gives a useful insight into the patterns which stories take, and a way to analyse the
   various steps of a hero's journey

FURTHER READING

Paul Cobley, *Narrative*, Routledge, 2003
  A clear and comprehensive guidebook to the forms of narrative from the earliest days to its current incarnations in new media

Sigmund Freud, *The Interpretation of Dreams* [1899], Penguin, 1991
  A book examining the symbolic meaning of dream images and providing examples of their interpretation

David Lodge, *The Art of Fiction*, Penguin, 1992
  A book that uses classic and modern fiction to explore the various methods and techniques used by writers

Jessie Matz, *The Modern Novel*, Blackwell, 2004
  A useful exploration of both modernism and postmodernism in literature

Michael McKeon (ed.), *Theory of the Novel: A Historical Approach*, Johns Hopkins University Press, 2000
  A collection of essays which provides a solid basis for understand the role of the novel and its place in the history of literature

Edward Said, *Orientalism*, Penguin [1978], 2003
  The classic text on post-colonialism

allegory a story or a situation with two different meanings, where the straightforward meaning on the surface is used to symbolise a deeper meaning underneath. This secondary meaning is often a spiritual or moral one whose values are represented by specific figures, characters or events in the narrative

allusion a passing reference in a work of literature to something outside the text; it may include other works of literature, myth, historical facts or biographical detail

compound sentence a sentence which contains one or more sub-clauses as well as the main clause

contemporary novel a novel set in the same time period in which the author wrote it

dialect a variety of speech, usually associated with geographical location, rather than social status; dialect covers vocabulary and syntax, accent covers the sound of the speech

dramatic tension when a series of events work together to create a need in the reader to find out what happens next

epistolary the method of telling a story through a series of letters, either from one person to another – giving a single perspective – or between many different participants, giving multiple individual viewpoints

first-person narrator a narrator who is involved in the story being told and can reveal only their own perspective, thoughts and feelings with no access to the thoughts and feelings of other characters

flashback a scene or event from the past which is related as an aside during a story set in the present

foreshadowing a literary technique whereby the author mentions events which are yet to be revealed in the narrative, either to increase dramatic tension, or to provide clues for the reader to attempt to guess what will happen next

historical novel a novel set in a time period prior to the time in which the author wrote it, in which the cultural/social/political events of that period play a significant part in the story

imagery descriptive language which uses images to make actions, objects and characters more vivid in the reader's mind. Metaphors and similes are examples of imagistic language

irony the humorous or sarcastic use of words to imply the opposite of what they normally mean; incongruity between what might be expected and what actually happens; the ill-timed arrival of an event that had been hoped for

juxtaposition the technique of placing two or more seemingly unrelated ideas next to each other in a text, creating meaning from the interaction of the differences and similarities between them

metaphor a figure of speech in which a word or phrase is applied to an object, a character or an action which does not literally belong to it, in order to imply a resemblance and create an unusual or striking image in the reader's mind

modernism a literary movement which moves away from traditional **realist** forms of writing to embrace experimental forms and a more personal perspective

motif a recurring idea in a work, which is used to draw the reader's attention to a particular theme or topic

narrative a story, tale or any recital of events, and the manner in which it is told. First-person narratives ('I') are told from the character's perspective and usually require the reader to judge carefully what is being said; second-person narratives ('you') suggest the reader is part of the story; in third-person narratives ('he', 'she', 'they') the **narrator** may be intrusive (continually commenting on the story), impersonal, or omniscient. More than one style of narrative may be used in a text

narrator the voice telling the story or relating a sequence of events

omniscient narrator a **narrator** who uses the third-person narrative and has a god-like knowledge of events and of the thoughts and feelings of the characters

pathetic fallacy the attribution of human feelings to objects in nature and, commonly, weather systems, so that the mood of the **narrator** or the characters can be discerned from the behaviour of the surrounding environment

post-colonialism a branch of literary theory which examines the texts written by authors from formerly colonised countries with regard to how the culture of such countries have been changed by colonisation and examining the process of recovery and regaining of cultural identity

postmodernism a literary movement which, in reaction to modernism, introduces more experimental ways of writing. Postmodern writing often plays with established forms as a way of commenting on them, or uses many different forms in a single work, mixing high and low culture, in an attempt to create a literature without boundaries

protagonist the principal character in a work of literature

realism a literary movement of the second half of the nineteenth century which attempted to depict everyday life in unromanticised terms, sometimes describing everyday activities in detail and attempting to tell stories of 'real' lives

stream of consciousness writing which presents thoughts as they occur to a character or **narrator** in a constant flow with no overt attempts to link or structure them

symbolism investing material objects with abstract powers and meanings greater than their own; allowing a complex idea to be represented by a single object

unreliable narrator a first-person **narrator** who does not necessarily always give the reader complete or accurate information, or whose personal feelings influence their interpretation of the events as narrated

Calum Kerr is a writer and lecturer. He has taught a variety of courses at Manchester Metropolitan University including Creative Writing, Fiction in English and Renaissance Drama, and has been a guest lecturer on other courses. He has published a wide range of stories, articles, reviews and papers.

YORK NOTES FOR GCSE AND KEY STAGE 3

GCSE

Maya Angelou
I Know Why the Caged Bird Sings

Jane Austen
Pride and Prejudice

Alan Ayckbourn
Absent Friends

Elizabeth Barrett Browning
Selected Poems

Robert Bolt
A Man for All Seasons

Harold Brighouse
Hobson's Choice

Charlotte Brontë
Jane Eyre

Emily Brontë
Wuthering Heights

Brian Clark
Whose Life is it Anyway?

Robert Cormier
Heroes

Shelagh Delaney
A Taste of Honey

Charles Dickens
David Copperfield
Great Expectations
Hard Times
Oliver Twist
Selected Stories

Roddy Doyle
Paddy Clarke Ha Ha Ha

George Eliot
The Mill on the Floss
Silas Marner

Anne Frank
The Diary of a Young Girl

William Golding
Lord of the Flies

Oliver Goldsmith
She Stoops to Conquer

Willis Hall
The Long and the Short and the Tall

Thomas Hardy
Far from the Madding Crowd
The Mayor of Casterbridge
Tess of the d'Urbervilles
The Withered Arm and other Wessex Tales

L. P. Hartley
The Go-Between

Seamus Heaney
Selected Poems

Susan Hill
I'm the King of the Castle

Barry Hines
A Kestrel for a Knave

Louise Lawrence
Children of the Dust

Harper Lee
To Kill a Mockingbird

Laurie Lee
Cider with Rosie

Arthur Miller
The Crucible
A View from the Bridge

Robert O'Brien
Z for Zachariah

Frank O'Connor
My Oedipus Complex and Other Stories

George Orwell
Animal Farm

J. B. Priestley
An Inspector Calls
When We Are Married

Willy Russell
Educating Rita
Our Day Out

J. D. Salinger
The Catcher in the Rye

William Shakespeare
Henry IV Part I
Henry V
Julius Caesar
Macbeth
The Merchant of Venice
A Midsummer Night's Dream
Much Ado About Nothing
Romeo and Juliet
The Tempest
Twelfth Night

George Bernard Shaw
Pygmalion

Mary Shelley
Frankenstein

R. C. Sherriff
Journey's End

Rukshana Smith
Salt on the snow

John Steinbeck
Of Mice and Men

Robert Louis Stevenson
Dr Jekyll and Mr Hyde

Jonathan Swift
Gulliver's Travels

Robert Swindells
Daz 4 Zoe

Mildred D. Taylor
Roll of Thunder, Hear My Cry

Mark Twain
Huckleberry Finn

James Watson
Talking in Whispers

Edith Wharton
Ethan Frome

William Wordsworth
Selected Poems

A Choice of Poets

Mystery Stories of the Nineteenth Century including The Signalman

Nineteenth Century Short Stories

Poetry of the First World War

Six Women Poets

For the AQA Anthology:

Duffy and Armitage & Pre-1914 Poetry

Heaney and Clarke & Pre-1914 Poetry

Poems from Different Cultures

Key Stage 3

William Shakespeare
Much Ado About Nothing
Richard III
The Tempest

Margaret Atwood
Cat's Eye
The Handmaid's Tale

Jane Austen
Emma
Mansfield Park
Persuasion
Pride and Prejudice
Sense and Sensibility

Pat Barker
Regeneration

William Blake
Songs of Innocence and of Experience

The Brontës
Selected Poems

Charlotte Brontë
Jane Eyre
Villette

Emily Brontë
Wuthering Heights

Angela Carter
The Bloody Chamber
Nights at the Circus
Wise Children

Geoffrey Chaucer
The Franklin's Prologue and Tale
The Merchant's Prologue and Tale
The Miller's Prologue and Tale
The Pardoner's Tale
The Prologue to the Canterbury Tales
The Wife of Bath's Prologue and Tale

Caryl Churchill
Top Girls

John Clare
Selected Poems

Joseph Conrad
Heart of Darkness

John Donne
Selected Poems

Charles Dickens
Bleak House
Great Expectations
Hard Times

Carol Ann Duffy
Selected Poems
The World's Wife

George Eliot
Middlemarch
The Mill on the Floss

T. S. Eliot
Selected Poems
The Waste Land

Sebastian Faulks
Birdsong

F. Scott Fitzgerald
The Great Gatsby

John Ford
'Tis Pity She's a Whore

John Fowles
The French Lieutenant's Woman

Michael Frayn
Spies

Charles Frazier
Cold Mountain

Brian Friel
Making History
Translations

William Golding
The Spire

Thomas Hardy
Jude the Obscure
The Mayor of Casterbridge
The Return of the Native
Selected Poems
Tess of the d'Urbervilles

Nathaniel Hawthorne
The Scarlet Letter

Homer
The Iliad
The Odyssey

Khaled Hosseini
The Kite Runner

Aldous Huxley
Brave New World

Henrik Ibsen
A Doll's House

James Joyce
Dubliners

John Keats
Selected Poems

Philip Larkin
High Windows
The Whitsun Weddings and Selected Poems

Ian McEwan
Atonement

Christopher Marlowe
Doctor Faustus
Edward II

Arthur Miller
All My Sons
Death of a Salesman

John Milton
Paradise Lost Books I and II

George Orwell
Nineteen Eighty-Four

Sylvia Plath
Selected Poems

William Shakespeare
Antony and Cleopatra
As You Like It
Hamlet
Henry IV Part I
King Lear
Macbeth
Measure for Measure
The Merchant of Venice
A Midsummer Night's Dream
Much Ado About Nothing
Othello
Richard II
Richard III
Romeo and Juliet
The Taming of the Shrew
The Tempest
Twelfth Night
The Winter's Tale

Mary Shelley
Frankenstein

Richard Brinsley Sheridan
The School for Scandal

Bram Stoker
Dracula

Alfred Tennyson
Selected Poems

Alice Walker
The Color Purple

Virgil
The Aeneid

John Webster
The Duchess of Malfi
The White Devil

Oscar Wilde
The Importance of Being Earnest
The Picture of Dorian Gray
A Woman of No Importance

Tennessee Williams
Cat on a Hot Tin Roof
The Glass Menagerie
A Streetcar Named Desire

Jeanette Winterson
Oranges Are Not the Only Fruit

Virginia Woolf
To the Lighthouse

William Wordsworth
The Prelude and Selected Poems

Wordsworth and Coleridge
Lyrical Ballads

Poetry of the First World War